KENNETH PATCHEN

An annotated, descriptive bibliography

KENNETH PATCHEN

KENNETH PATCHEN

An annotated, descriptive bibliography
with cross-referenced index

by

RICHARD G. MORGAN
East Tennessee State University

Foreword by
LAWRENCE FERLINGHETTI

PAUL P. APPEL, Publisher
Mamaroneck, New York

Library of Congress Cataloging in Publication Data

Morgan, Richard G
  Kenneth Patchen.
  1. Patchen, Kenneth, 1911-1972—Bibliography.
  z8663.6.M67 (PS3531.A764) 016.811'5'4 78-15376
  ISBN 0-911858-36-9

Printed in the United States of America

THIS BOOK

is for all the creatures of the world, particularly those who have been brutalized by the barbarism and cruelty of the human race; for every dog and cat now in a city pound, without love or care, awaiting a horrible death; for every animal crushed on the highways or starving in the streets of the world; for every animal tortured in scientific experiments, with no hope of an end to its suffering except a death which is both painful and unnecessary; for every creature killed to satisfy people's taste for flesh; for all creatures from the smallest to the largest, who have suffered or who are now suffering from human sadism, carelessness, or stupidity.

TO THEM IS THIS BOOK DEDICATED

TABLE OF CONTENTS

LIST OF ILLUSTRATIONS

Photographs of Patchen Books are by Richard G. Morgan

A FOREWARNED WORD

Reader, do not enter here expecting to find the still hot heart of the poet. Here are no more than his bones, stripped by time. It is strange to see this bare-bones record here laid out, the orgasms between poems and the agonies between them left out. One must read between these lines for the real life of him, in this fine key to everything he put to paper. Cold this bibliographic hieroglyph, yet still passionate and compassionate the poetry itself to which this book guides you, like some bibliophile Virgil leading us through the illuminated inferno of Patchen's world.

Lawrence Ferlinghetti
February 1978

This bibliography is a record of works by and about Kenneth Patchen, American poet, novelist, and artist (1911-1972). I have structured the work in the way I feel will maximize easy use and consultation. Before the main body of the bibliography, there is a chronology which places each of Patchen's works in a biographical framework, and at the conclusion of the work an index.

The descriptive method is based on Donald Gallup's adaptation of the American Library Association system, "which ignores blanks and leaves containing only advertisements, in order to account for all leaves, although blank pages are not mentioned."[1] The method functions as follows:

The general rule is that when the unnumbered printed preliminary leaves count up (as pages) to the first numbered page of the book, these leaves are not specified in the collation. When they do not count up, they are specified: *e.g.* 1 blank leaf, 3 leaves, 8-29 pp., because here the *printed* preliminary material counts up to only six pages. When the first numbered page is the verso of a leaf unnumbered on the recto, the number of the recto is supplied in square brackets: *e.g.*, 1 blank leaf, 3 leaves, [9]-29 pp., thus indicating that 10 is the first page numbered. The collation "29 pp." alone indicates that the preliminary material counts up to the first numbered page and that the text ends on a page numbered 29 (page [30], being blank, is not specified). The collation "29 [1] pp.", on the other hand, indicates either that the text ends on the unnumbered page [30], or that a colophon, index , or some other printed material appears on that page. "29 pp., a leaf" indicates that the text ends on page 29 and that additional material not a continuation of the text appears on a final unnumbered leaf, either the recto or verso or both being printed.[2]

Information on particular sections follows.

Section A: Works are treated in full descriptive detail. Both American and British editions are described, with foreign reprints not in the English language merely enumerated within the proper entry, except in cases where they assume unusual importance. Special copies, which exist for many of the books, are described individually within the entries.

[1]Donald Gallup, *A Bibliography of Ezra Pound* (London: Rupert Hart-Davis, 1963) p. 9
[2]Ibid., pp. 9-10.

Section B: Due to the ephemeral or private nature of many of these items, complete publication data was not always available, and when available was sometimes dependent upon the recollections of individuals without corroborating records.

Section C: Anthology appearances, when they involved merely the reprinting of previously published material, have not been included.

Sections A-C: Descriptions are based on examination of copies of the books or pamphlets themselves, and whenever possible, multiple copies, supplemented by information drawn from publishers, the author's relatives, and others.

Section D: Although an attempt has been made to make this section comprehensive, including reprints of Patchen's work in periodicals, the fugitive nature of many publications creates the possibility that there may be omissions. As every effort was made to check the section against records kept by the author's widow, and periodical files in the Patchen Archive at the University of California at Santa Cruz, if omissions exist, they are certainly few in number. The same should be noted for sections J and K.

Section K: Please see note at beginning of section.

Section L: In all cases where it was possible, letters written by Patchen or his wife have been described by date, type (holograph or typewritten), length, and return address, and letters to Patchen described by date, type, and length. In a few cases where the collection in question was uncatalogued, and neither a photocopy nor specific information was obtainable from the owner, the item has been described only in general terms.

Section M: Please see note at beginning of section.

Index: the index identifies book titles (in capital letters), other titles (in quotation marks), periodicals (in italics), publishers (regular upper and lower case letters), and authors other than Patchen (regular letters). Each appearance in any of these categories in the bibliography is noted, in the order in which it appears in the bibliography, by the number of the item in which it appears.

The bibliography includes all known items through the end of the calendar year 1977.

ACKNOWLEDGEMENTS

The following have all been important to me in the progress of this work. To single any out would be to diminish the rest, so I merely present their names, with my gratitude.

Paul P. Appel, Gloria Baca, Misty M.M. Bee, Millicent Bell, Lynn Bloom, Rita Bottoms, Richard Cary, Momma Cat, Chippers, Margaret Coffey, Jack Conroy, Morris Eaves, Elvira, David Farmer, Lawrence Ferlinghetti, June Fischer, Lissa Fischer, Robert Fischer, Willy Fischer, Robert Fleming, Brad Hayden, Hamlin Hill, Leon Howard, Inter-library loan at the University of New Mexico, the administrative staff of Harding High School in Warren, Ohio, Elfrieda Lang, James Laughlin, Russell Maylone, Edward Mitchell, Fern McLean, Moonshadow, Griselda Ohannessian, Miriam Patchen, Bern Porter, Richard Power, Jon Reinschreiber, Alphonse Lothar Rule, Tessie Segal, Helen Sharlach, Jerry Sharlach, Susan Scharlach, Sarah Sherman, Keitha Shoupe, Saundra Taylor, James Thorson, Donald Van Greenby, Sheri Van Greenby, the Ludwig Vogelstein Foundation, Neda Westlake, Hugh Witemeyer, Brooke Whiting, Mary Janzen Wilson, Joseph Zavadil.

CHRONOLOGY

1911	Kenneth Frederick Patchen is born on December 13 in Niles, Ohio, to Wayne and Eva McQuade Patchen. He is the third child, preceded by Eunice (born in 1902, died in a flu epidemic in 1913) and Hugh (born in 1903). The family is lower-middle-class economically, its members primarily coal miners and steel mill workers of Scotch and Irish ancestry.
1914	Majel Patchen is born on July 21.
1916	Kathleen Patchen is born; the family moves to Warren, Ohio, where Kenneth enters elementary school.
1920	The last child, Ruth, is born on January 22.
1923	Patchen starts a diary and writes his first poems.
1924	Enters East Junior High School in Warren.
1925	Kathleen is killed on her way to church by a car which jumps the sidewalk.
1926	Enters Warren G. Harding High School in Warren.
1926-1929	Active in many school activities including football, track, debate, school newspaper. Editor of the yearbook, *Echoes*, in 1929. His first publications, six poems in the school newspaper, *High School Life*, in 1928 and 1929.
1929	Spends the summer working in the steel mills. The family, which had become relatively prosperous, is now destitute.
1929-1930	Scholarship student at Alexander Meikeljohn's Experimental College at the University of Wisconsin.
1930	Attends Commonwealth College in Mena, Arkansas for several months. This marks the end of his formal education.
1930-1933	Travels around the United States and Canada taking odd jobs, including farm laborer, gardener, hiking shelter caretaker, and janitor. Spends several months in New York City.
1932	First regular publication, "Permanence," a sonnet, in the *New York Times*.

3

1933   Lives in Boston, where he is befriended by Conrad Aiken, John Wheelright, Malcolm Cowley, and others. At a party on Christmas Eve, he meets a young student, Miriam Oikemus, determining almost immediately to marry her.

1934   Works in a rubber plant near Boston, where he develops a severe sinus condition which necessitates an operation. Continues to correspond with Miriam; in the spring, they leave Boston for New York. Soon after, they go to Ohio, where they marry on June 28, a union which was to last Patchen's entire life. They move back to New York. Begins reviewing books for *New Republic*.

1935   Lives in New York City. Works on W.P.A. New York Guide. Receives a book contract from Random House. Goes to Rhinebeck, New York for several months to write *Before the Brave*.

1936   First book, *Before the Brave,* is published by Random House, reviewed by over fifty publications. Awarded Guggenheim Fellowship. Moves to Phoenix, Arizona, then Sante Fe, New Mexico.

1937   Moves to Los Angeles. Suffers disabling back injury.

1937-1938   Lives in Los Angeles, working on movie scripts. Works on W.P.A. California Guide.

1939   Spends time in Concord, Massachusetts. *First Will and Testament* published by James Laughlin's New Directions publishing company. Moves to Norfolk, Connecticut, where he and Miriam become, respectively, the accounting and shipping departments of New Directions.

1940   Moves to New York City. Begins to write *The Journal of Albion Moonlight*. Associates with Henry Miller, E.E. Cummings, Maxwell Bodenheim, and others.

1941   Unable to find a publisher who will risk bringing it out, the Patchens publish *The Journal of Albion Moonlight* by subscription. It is printed by Peter Beilenson at the Walpole Printing Office in Mount Vernon, New York, and "launched" at the Gotham

Book Mart in New York City, whose owner, Frances Steloff, has purchased the entire trade edition of the book.

1942   *The Dark Kingdom*, the limited edition of which is the first of the "painted books," each carrying a different original work painted onto the cover by Patchen, is brought out by Harriss and Givens, their first and last book. *The Teeth of the Lion* is published in New Directions' "Poet of the Month" series. *The City Wears a Slouch Hat*, a radio play, is produced on Columbia Radio Workshop.

1943   Harper publishes *Cloth of the Tempest*.

1944   Visits Concord, Massachusetts. Receives Ohioana Award for *Cloth of the Tempest*.

1945   *Memoirs of a Shy Pornographer* (New Directions).

1946   Spends the summer in Mount Pleasant, then returns to New York City. *An Astonished Eye* (Untide Press), *Outlaw of the Lowest Planet* (Grey Walls Press), *Panels for the Walls of Heaven* (Bern Porter), *The Selected Poems* (New Directions), *Sleepers Awake* (Padell), *They Keep Riding Down All the Time* (Padell), *Pictures of Life and of Death* (Padell) are all published. Padell also reprints *The Journal of Albion Moonlight* and other works.

1947   Moves to a house in Old Lyme, Connecticut, where he and Miriam remain for several years.

1948   *See You in the Morning* (Padell), Patchen's only "conventional" novel is published. *To Say If You Love Someone* (Decker) printed. *CCCLXXIV Poems* brought out by Padell, along with several reprints.

1950   First major operation on spine. Many benefit readings and concerts to raise money, through a fund headed by T.S. Eliot, Thornton Wilder, Archibald MacLeish, W.H. Auden, E.E. Cummings, Marianne Moore, William Carlos Williams, Edith Sitwell, and others.

1951   Moves to west coast for health reasons.

1952   Settles in San Francisco. *Orchards, Thrones, and Caravans* (The Print Workshop).

1953   *Fables and Other Little Tales* (Jargon).

1954   Receives Shelley Memorial Award. The City Lights Bookshop publishes *Poems of Humor and Protest* in their "Pocket Poets" series. *The Famous Boating Party* (New Directions).

1955   *Glory Never Guesses,* a silkscreen portfolio of picture-poems, is brought out.

1956   Moves to Palo Alto, California. Spends much time at the Palo Alto Clinic, finally undergoing a spinal fusion operation, which gives him some relief from pain for the first time in almost twenty years. The Patchens buy a house at 2340 Sierra Court in Palo Alto, the first place they have owned, and their final home. *Surprise for the Bagpipe Player*, another silkscreen portfilio, is produced.

1957   Begins the poetry-and-jazz movement, reading with jazz groups up and down the west coast until 1959. *Hurrah for Anything* (Jargon), *Kenneth Patchen Reads With the Chamber Jazz Sextet* (Cadence—recording), *When We Were Here Together* (New Directions), and *The Selected Poems, Enlarged Edition* (New Directions).

1958   *Poemscapes* (Jargon).

1959   A surgical "mishap" destroys the benefits of the 1956 operation, leaving Patchen in great pain, and rendering him almost completely bedridden for the rest of his life. *Don't Look Now,* his only full-length play, produced by the Troupe Theatre in Palo Alto. *Kenneth Patchen Reads His Selected Poems* (Folkways—recording), *Kenneth Patchen Reads With Jazz in Canada* (Folksways—recording).

1960   *Because It Is* (New Directions) and *The Love Poems* (City Lights). *The Moment*, a bound edition of *Glory Never Guesses* and *Surprise for the Bagpipe Player* is brought out.

1961   *Kenneth Patchen Reads His Love Poems* (Folkways—recording).

1966　　*Hallelujah Anyway* (New Directions). *Double-header* (New Directions).

1967　　Receives $10,000 award from the National Foundation on the Arts and Humanities for "life-long contribution to American letters."

1968　　*The Collected Poems of Kenneth Patchen* (New Directions), *But Even So* (New Directions), *Love & War Poems* (Whisper & Shout).

1970　　*Aflame and Afun of Walking Faces* (New Directions), *There's Love All Day* (Hallmark).

1971　　*Wonderings* (New Directions), *Tell You That I Love You* (Hallmark).

1972　　Dies on January 8. *In Quest of Candlelighters* (New Directions), *Patchen's Funny Fables* (Greentree—recording), *The Journal of Albion Moonlight* (Folkways—recording).

1977　　*Patchen's Lost Plays* [*Don't Look Now* and *The City Wears a Slouch Hat*] (Capra Press).

BY PATCHEN

1. BEFORE THE BRAVE (1936) Poetry.
2. FIRST WILL AND TESTAMENT (1939) Poetry.
3. THE JOURNAL OF ALBION MOONLIGHT (1941) Prose.
4. THE DARK KINGDOM (1942) Poetry.
5. THE TEETH OF THE LION (1942) Poetry.
6. CLOTH OF THE TEMPEST (1943) Poetry.
7. MEMOIRS OF A SHY PORNOGRAPHER (1945) Prose.
8. AN ASTONISHED EYE LOOKS OUT OF THE AIR ([1945] 1946) Poetry.
9. OUTLAW OF THE LOWEST PLANET (1946) Poetry.
10. THE SELECTED POEMS (1946) Poetry.
11. SLEEPERS AWAKE (1946) Prose.
12. PANELS FOR THE WALLS OF HEAVEN (1946) Prose-poems.
13. PICTURES OF LIFE AND OF DEATH (1946) Poetry.
14. THEY KEEP RIDING DOWN ALL THE TIME (1946-7) Prose.
15. CCCLXXIV POEMS (1947-8) Poetry.
16. SEE YOU IN THE MORNING (1947) Prose.
17. TO SAY IF YOU LOVE SOMEONE (1948) Poetry.
18. RED WINE AND YELLOW HAIR (1949) Poetry.
19. IN PEACEABLE CAVES (1950) Poetry.
20. ORCHARDS, THRONES & CARAVANS (1952) Poetry.
21. FABLES AND OTHER LITTLE TALES (1953) Prose-poems.
22. THE FAMOUS BOATING PARTY (1954) Poetry.
23. POEMS OF HUMOR & PROTEST (1954) Poetry.
24. GLORY NEVER GUESSES (1955) Picture-poems.
25. SURPRISE FOR THE BAGPIPE PLAYER (1956) Picture-poems.
26. HURRAH FOR ANYTHING (1957) Poetry.
27. WHEN WE WERE HERE TOGETHER (1957) Poetry.

28. POEMSCAPES (1958) Prose-poems.

29. BECAUSE IT IS (1960) Poetry.

30. THE MOMENT (1960) Picture-poems.

31. THE LOVE POEMS (1960) Poetry.

32. DOUBLEHEADER (1966) Prose; prose-poems.

33. HALLELUJAH ANYWAY (1966) Picture-poems.

34. THE COLLECTED POEMS (1968) Poetry.

35. BUT EVEN SO (1968) Picture-poems.

36. LOVE & WAR POEMS (1968) Poetry; prose; drawings.

37. SELECTED POEMS [U.K.] (1968) Poetry.

38. AFLAME AND AFUN OF WALKING FACES (1947) Poems and drawings.

39. THERE'S LOVE ALL DAY (1970) Poetry.

40. WONDERINGS (1971) Picture-poems.

41. TELL YOU THAT I LOVE YOU (1971) Poetry.

42. IN QUEST OF CANDLELIGHTERS (1972) Prose.

43. PATCHEN'S LOST PLAYS (1977) Drama.

A1   BEFORE THE BRAVE   1936

a. *First Edition*

[Decorative device: in black] / [In red:] BEFORE / THE BRAVE /
BY / KENNETH / PATCHEN / RANDOM HOUSE / NEW
YORK / [Decorative device: in black]

131 pp. 24 x 16 cm. Red cloth with black lettering [with gold decorative devices
identical to those on the title page above and below the title]. Light tan dust-
wrapper with red lettering and black design.

Published in January at $2.00; 2000 copies printed at the Walpole Printing
Office, Mount Vernon, New York.

Contents: INTRODUCTION: when in the course of human events—among
ourselves and with all nations—it is for us the living—shall not perish from
the earth—the last full measure of devotion—that we here highly resolve—it is
the right of the people—we mutually pledge to each other—that to secure these
rights—we hold these truths to be self-evident—the world will little note—to
provide new guards for future security—thus far so nobly advanced—WE
BRING NO BOXED SOLUTION;OUR FLAGS STREAM OUT FOR USE,
NOT TRUMPET—MASSES: The Magic Car—The Temple in Red Square—
A Letter to a Distant Relative—Prayer to Go to Paridise with the Asses—An
Invitation to the Dance—A Letter to a Policeman in Kansas City—There's a
Train Leaving Soon—1935—THE EARTH'S LUTE, THE SHINING
HEART: Let Us Have Madness—We Leave You Pleasure—A Letter to the
Citizens of Tomorrow—History is a Throne and a Gate—Demonstration—
The Other Side: The Green Home—A Letter to Those Who Are About to Die—
The Ladder—The Red Woman—A Little Ode—OVER OUR FACES THE
HUSHED APPLAUSE, THE WALL OF WORDS THAT NEARLY
KILLED: Letter to the Old Men—Loyalty Is the Life You Are—Night Has
Been as Beautiful as Virginia—The Firing—This Man Was Your Brother—
My Generation Reading the Newspapers—A Letter on the Use of Machine
Guns at Weddings—AND SOMETHING STABS INTO THE SUN BEFORE
OUR OPENED EYES: All the Day—Nocturne for the Heirs of Light—A
Letter on Liberty—A Letter to the Liberals—We Must Be Slow—Dostoyevsky
—Note for a Diary (One and Two)—HOW WHITE, HOW CALM THE
HOURS ARE: Ode to the New Men—Fields of Earth—A Letter to the In-
ventors of a Tradition—The Mechanical Heart—Ark: Angelus: Anvil—The
Stranger—Graduation—Having Been Near—Country Excursion—OUR
EYES ARE THE EYES AT YOUR WINDOWS GENTLEMEN/ OUR
HANDS ARE THE HANDS AT THE LATCHES OF YOUR DOORS:
Leaflet (One)—Leaflet (Two)—Poem in the Form of Letter: To Lauro de
Bosis—A Letter to the Young Men—WE HEAR THE DARK CURVE OF
ETERNITY GO COUGHING DOWN THE HILLS: Class of 1934—This
Early Day—The Movable Journey—Pick up the Evening Paper—A Letter
on Thanksgiving—THE TIMELESS BRIDE OF ALL OUR LOVING: Fare-
well to the Bluewoman—Joe Hill Listens to the Praying—Pinning the Tail
on the Donkey—Chant: Not a Solo but a Scene of Action—The Trial: A Mixed
Chorus and Choice of Voices—A World Whose Sun Retreats Before the Brave

b. *Second Edition* (1974)

BEFORE / THE BRAVE / BY / KENNETH / PATCHEN /
[Publisher's Device] / HASKELL HOUSE PUBLISHERS LTD. /
PUBLISHERS OF SCARCE SCHOLARLY BOOKS / NEW
YORK, N.Y. 10012 / 1974

131 pp. 19.5 x 13.5 cm. Blue cloth with gold lettering.

Photo-offset from the first edition, reduced in size. Contents identical.

Note: According to Miriam Patchen, Random House neglected to renew the
copyright in 1964, thus putting the entire work in the public domain. Despite
efforts to block reprinting of the work by Haskell House, there were no legal
restrictions to prevent them from doing so.

A2   FIRST WILL AND TESTAMENT   1939

a. *First Edition*

[In black:] KENNETH PATCHEN / [In red:] FIRST WILL &
TESTAMENT / [In black:] NEW DIRECTIONS • NORFOLK
• CONN.

181 [1] pp. 24 x 17.5 cm. Red cloth with gold lettering. Yellow and red dust-
wrapper with red and black lettering.

Published November 7th at $2.50. *Colophon:* "Eight hundred copies . . . were
printed for New Directions at the Walpole printing office in July and August
1939." Book and jacket design by Peter Beilenson.

Contents: All That Night Lights Were Seen Moving in Every Direction—All
the Bright Foam of Talk—And He Had Wilder Moments—And in Another
Place Uses the Same Phrase—And What with the Blunders—A Revolutionary
Prayer—A Small But Brilliant Fire Blazed in the Grate—As She Was Thus
Alone in the Clear Moonlight—At the Sound of My Voice—Autumn Is the
Crow's Time—Avarice and Ambition Only Were the First Builders of Towns
and Founders of Empire—Behold, One of Several Little Christs—Biography
of Southern Rain—Boxers Hit Harder When Women Are Around—But the
Images of His Former Dreams Still Haunted Him—Can the Harp Shoot
Through Its Propellers?—Career for a Child of Five—Creation—Crossing on
Staten Island Ferry—Death Will Amuse Them—Do the Dead Know What
Time It Is?—Early in the Morning—Eight Early Poems: I, II, III The Sea Has
Caves and Urns, IV, V, VI Fragment from "A Schoolboy's Odyssey", VII Geog-
raphy of Music, VIII At the New Year— Elegy for the Silent Voices and the
Joiners of Everything—Eve of St. Agony or The Middleclass Was Sitting on

Its Fat—Fall of the Evening Star—Fifth Dimension—Fog—Harrowed by
These Apprehensions He Resolved to Commit Himself to the Mercy of the
Storm—He Did Cry to Them at Last with All His Lungs—Heine Lived in Ger-
many—He Is Guarded by Crowds and Shackled with Formalities—He Thought
of Mad Ellen's Ravings and of The Wretched Skeleton on the Rock—He Was
Alone (As in Reality) upon His Humble Bed—How Different the Expression
of This Face!—Hymn to a Trench Gun— I Can't Understand!—I Don't Want to
Startle You—If We Are to Know Where We Live—I Got the Fat Poet into a
Corner—Inasmuch As War Is Not for Women—I Never Had Any Other Desire
So Strong—In Judgment of the Leaf—In Memory of Kathleen—I Suddenly
Became Conscious That This Thing Was Looking at Me Intently—Man Is to
Man a Beast—Meditation of My Lady of Sorrows—Nice Day for a Lynching—
Niobe—On the South-west Coast of Erehwemos Stands a Romantic Little
Village—Outside Looking Outside—Palms for a Catholic Child—Peter's
Diary in Goodentown: Peter Records the Sparrow's Falling Feather, The Day-
Mists Are Strewn with Us, Spring in Goodentown, Forest Near Goodentown,
Peter Reads Emerson, Bya Deena, Peter Gains a Son, Peter Reports on Him-
self, Peter's Little Daughter Dies, The Shelling of Goodentown—Plow Horses
—Poem—Poem Written after Reading Certain Poets Sired by the English
School and Bitched by the C.P.—Portrait on an American Theme—Religion
Is That I Love You—She Had Concealed Him in a Deep Dark Cave—Stayed
No Longer in the Place Than to Hire a Guide for the Next Stage—Street Corner
College—The Black Panther and the Little Boy—The Body Beside the Ties—
The Character of Love Seen as a Search for the Lost—The Deer and the Snake
—The Executions in Moscow—The Figure Motioned with Its Mangled Hand
Towards the Wall Behind It—The Fox—The Hangman's Great Hands—The
Old Lean Over the Tombstones—The Overworld—The Place We Were In Was
a Small Square room with a Partial Roof—The Poor Child with the Hooked
Hands—The Quantity of Mercy—The Queer Client and the Forest Inn—"These
Have Gone with Silent Hands, Seeking"—The Soldier and the Star—The State
of the Nation—Though I Had Much More to Say—Tomorrow—To Whom It
May Concern—23rd Street Runs Into Heaven—When You Come to the End—
You May All Go Home Now

Note: At end of contents: "A few of the longer titles are paraphrased versions
of prose selections from certain writers of the 17th and 18th Centuries."

b. *Second Edition* (1948)

FIRST WILL / [superimposed on an &:] KENNETH PATCHEN /
TESTAMENT [New York: Padell]

1 blank leaf, 3 leaves, 9-177 pp., 1 blank leaf. 22.5 x 14.5 cm. Red cloth with black
and gold lettering. Light grey dust-wrapper with blue and black lettering.

Published in May at $2.25, later $2.50. 2500 copies printed. *On verso of title-
leaf:* "Published by Padell, 830 Broadway, New York / Printed and Bound in
the United States by Ganis and Harris, New York."

Contents: Adds photograph of the Patchens, dated 1946, and a new poem—
"for Miriam (As frothing wounds of roses)," dated January 27, 1948, immediately following copyright leaf. Otherwise same as first edition.

Note: Immediately preceding the title-leaf, appears the following list of places
where Patchen wrote his books: *Pictures Of Life And Of Death* (written in
Greenwich Village); *The Journal of Albion Moonlight* (. . . 81 Bleecker St., New
York City); *An Astonished Eye Looks Out Of The Air* (. . . Mt. Pleasant, New
York); *Before The Brave* (. . . Warren, Ohio—Rhinebeck, New York); *Cloth Of
The Tempest* (. . . Greenwich Village); *They Keep Riding Down All The Time*
(. . . Mt. Pleasant, New York); *See You In The Morning* (. . . Connecticut);
Sleepers Awake (. . . Greenwich Village); *First Will & Testament* (. . . Santa Fe—
Los Angeles—Concord, Mass.); *Selected Poems; Memoirs Of A Shy Pornog-
rapher* (. . . West 22nd St., New York City); *Panels for The Walls of Heaven*
(. . . Greenwich Village); *The Teeth Of The Lion* (. . . Morun Falls, North Da-
ponta [sic]); *The Dark Kingdom* (. . . Avenue A, at 16th St., New York City).

A3   THE JOURNAL OF ALBION MOONLIGHT   1941

a. *First Edition, first issue (subscribers edition)*

[Title page consists of two facing pages. First, in black:] The JOUR-
NAL / OF ALBION / MOONLIGHT / [In red: decorative rule] /
[In black: decorative rule] / [In red:] KENNETH / PATCHEN /
[Second page, in red:] The JOURNAL / OF ALBION / MOON-
LIGHT / [In black: decorative rule] / [In red: decorative rule] /
[In black:] KENNETH / PATCHEN [New York: Kenneth Patchen]

3 blank leaves, 1 leaf, 313 pp., 1 leaf. 24.5 x 17.5 cm. Handmade Italian rag-laid
paper, 3/4-leather binding with buckram spine stamped in gold, and black
slipcase with red and black label. Numbered and signed.

Published (presubscribed) in June at $10.00. 50 copies printed at the Walpole
Printing Office, Mount Vernon, New York. Printed and designed by Peter
Beilenson [zodiacal devices by W.A. Dwiggens].

Note: The book was originally announced for publication on January 26 by
New Directions, in their catalogue for Winter 1941-1942. When New Directions
decided suddenly not to publish it after all, and another publisher could not be
found, the Patchens published and marketed it themselves, by subscription
and general sale.

b. *First Edition, second issue (regular edition)*

Title-pages, pagination, and size as first issue. Bound in black linen with red
label with gold design on front cover and spine. Red, white and black dust-
wrapper with white lettering. Numbered and signed.

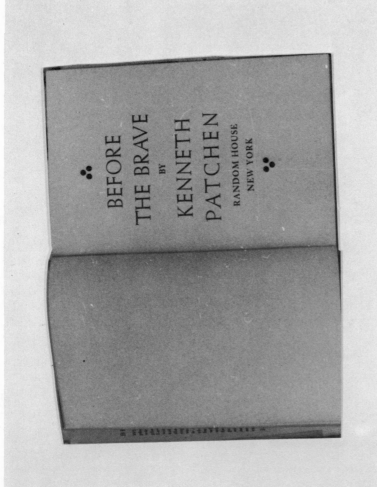

Title Page of *Before the Brave* (1936). Ala.

Title Pages of *The Journal of Albion Moonlight* (1941). A3b.

Published in July at $5.00. 295 copies printed at the Walpole Printing Office.

Note: Almost the entire issue was purchased as a lot by the Gotham Book Mart.

c. *First Trade Edition* (1944)

The JOURNAL / OF ALBION / MOONLIGHT / [Double decorative rule] / KENNETH / PATCHEN / New York / [black dot] / THE UNITED BOOK GUILD / [black dot] / 1944

> 1 blank leaf, 2 leaves, 313 pp., 1 blank leaf. 23.75 x 16 cm. Red and black paper boards with white lettering. Dust-jacket identical to book covers.

> Published in September at $3.00. 3000 copies printed.

d. *Second Trade Edition, first impression* (1946)

[In black lettering, inside solid red oval:] THE / JOURNAL / OF / ALBION / MOONLIGHT / KENNETH / PATCHEN / [Below oval:] / PADELL / [large space] / NEW YORK / [Between two previous terms, on next line:] MCMXLV

> 1 blank leaf, 3 leaves, 313 pp., 1 blank leaf. 23 x 15.5 cm. Red cloth with gold lettering. Red, black, and yellow dust jacket with alternate red, black, and yellow lettering.

> Published in March at $3.00. 1500 copies printed. *On verso of title-leaf:* Fourth Edition 1946.

e. *Second Trade Edition, second impression* (1947)

> As (d). *on verso of title-leaf:* Fifth Edition 1946. Published in January 1947 at $3.00. 3000 copies printed.

f. *First Paperback Edition* (1961)

The JOURNAL / OF ALBION / MOONLIGHT / [Double decorative rule] / KENNETH / PATCHEN [New York: New Directions Publishing Corp.]

> 3 leaves, 313 pp. 20.25 x 13.5 cm. Stiff black paper wrappers with gray and white lettering.

Published August 29 at $1.65. 6500 copies. *On verso of title-leaf:* "First published as New Directions Paperbook No. 99, 1961." Later printings (eight to date) are identified as such on the verso of the title-leaf.

Notes: Photo-offset from original 1941 edition. The cover drawing was done by Patchen specifically for this edition.

g. *German edition* (1963)

Wiesbaden: Limes Verlag, 1963.

h. *First Dutch Edition* (1965)

Amsterdam: Uitgerverij De Dezige Bij, 1965.

i. *Second Dutch Edition* (1967)

Amsterdam: J.M. Meulenhoff, 1967.

A4   THE DARK KINGDOM   1942

a. *First edition, regular issue*

[Title page consists of two facing pages. First, in red:] The Dark Kingdom / [In black:] KENNETH PATCHEN / [Second page, in red:] stands [In black:] ABOVE THE WATERS AS A SENTI-NEL / WARNING MAN OF DANGER FROM HIS / OWN KIND. ON ITS ALTARS THE DEEDS OF / BLOOD ARE NOT OFFERED; HERE ARE / WATCHERS WHOSE EYES ARE FIXED ON / THE ETERNAL UNDER-TAKINGS OF THE / SPIRIT. WHAT HAS BEEN COMMON AND / TARNISHED IN THESE POOR WOMBS, / HERE PARTAKES OF IMMOR-TALITY. IN / ITS WINDOWS ARE REFLECTED THE UN- / RETURNING EVENTS OF CHILDHOOD. ALL / WHO ASK LIFE, FIND A PEACE EVERLAST- / ING IN ITS RADIANT HALLS. ALL WHO / HAVE OPPOSED IN SECRET, ARE HERE / PROVIDED WITH GREEN CROWNS. ALL / WHO HAVE BEEN DRAGGED THROUGH / THE COWLED FLAME OF THIS WORLD, / ARE HERE CLOTHED IN THE BRIGHT RAI- / MENT OF THE TEMPEST. HERE ALL WHO / SORROW AND ARE WEARY UNDER / STRANGE

BURDENS—FEARING DEATH, / ARE SEEN TO ENTER THE WHITE THRONE / ROOM OF GOD / HARRISS & GIVENS [Black dot] New York [Device, in red. Picture of a satyr within a circle]

2 blank leaves, 6 leaves, 9-117 pp., 1 leaf, 1 blank leaf. 24.5 x 16.5 cm. Dark blue cloth with gold lettering. Black dust-wrapper with white lettering and design.

Published on January 29 at $2.25. 775 copies printed in December and January. *Colophon*: "Seven hundred seventy-five copies / of this edition of THE DARK KINGDOM / have been printed on Arak paper / for Harriss and Givens at the / Walpole Printing Office / Design and typography by / Kenneth Patchen."

Contents: The Watcher—The Forms of Knowledge—The Rites of Darkness— The Second People—The Cloth of the Tempest—The Village Tudda— Irkalla's White Caves—The Lasting Seasons—These Unreturning Destinies—Meben— Fellow Soul, Sound Hunting to Thy Immeasurable Heart—A Temple—A Devotion—The Manifold Fusions—Heaven and Earth—'Into Another Mission'— The Naked Land—The Crowded Net—Paxdominisit Sem Pervobiscum Etcumspiri Tutuo—The Meaning of Life—Continuation of the Landscape—'For Losing Her Love All Would I Profane'—'We Go Out Together into the Staring Town'—'From My High Love I Look at that Poor World There'—'Where My Stag-Antlered Love Moves'—'As We Are So Wonderfully Done With Each Other'—Cathy—Like a Mourningless Child—'There Is Nothing False in Thee'—The Expectant Shelters—The Wolf of Winter—Virtue—You Are Not Worthy, Lord—'In the Footsteps of the Walking Air'—What the Grecian Earns—'I Suggest That This Day Be Made Holy'—How God Was Made—The Known Soldier—Lenada—The Intimate Guest—The Handmaidens of Nobanna—The Spirit of Place—Digging for Clams—Waking Into Sleep—Canticle of Pilkes Ludd—What Happened in the Camps—Oniiasy—In Your Body All Bodies Lie—Pastoral—Those Upon Whom God Has Labored—An Examination into Life and Death—'Our Chief Amusement Was to Lie Naked'— Saturday Night in the Parthenon—The Outlaw of the Lowest Planet—The Climate of War—Little Bear—The Permanent Migrations—Preparation for the Highest Being—There Is One Who Watches

Note: Wayne Harriss and Jan Givens were students at Columbia University and Wellesley College respectively when they began their publishing venture. THE DARK KINGDOM was the only book they produced.

b. *First Edition, special (painted) issue*

Title page, pagination, contents, and size a regular issue.

Published January 1942. 75 copies available at $5.00. Bound in French-fold paper and slipcased. Each carried an original watercolor painted by the author pasted onto the cover. Numbered and signed, with a slipcase identical to the dust-wrapper of the regular issue.

Note: These were the first of Patchen's "painted books;" he eventually did over one thousand of them. The covers were sometimes stripped to bare boards, sometimes covered with Japanese or other special papers, sometimes left as is. Painting materials were equally varied—water colors, inks, injection of cloth dies into wet casein, gouache, vegetable compounds and rubber cement, etc. Occasionally the front and back covers formed a single work in an extension—relationship; at other times they were separate paintings. Each painting, whatever its nature, was a different, individual, one-of-a-kind creation.

c. *Second Edition* (1948)

[Lettering in white, against a black background:] THE DARK KINGDOM [Picture of headless bird, partially obscuring letters G and D in KINGDOM] STANDS / ABOVE THE WATERS AS A SENTINEL / WARNING MAN OF DANGER FROM HIS / OWN KIND. ON ITS ALTARS THE DEEDS / OF BLOOD ARE NOT OFFERED; HERE / ARE WATCHERS WHOSE EYES ARE / FIXED ON THE ETERNAL UNDER-TAKINGS / OF THE SPIRIT. WHAT HAS BEEN COM- / MON AND TARNISHED IN THESE POOR / WOMBS, HERE PARTAKES OF IMMORTAL- / ITY. IN ITS WINDOWS ARE REFLECTED / THE UNRETURNING EVENTS OF CHILD- / HOOD. ALL WHO ASK LIFE, FIND A / PEACE EVER-LASTING IN ITS RADIANT / HALLS. ALL WHO HAVE OPPOSED IN / SECRET [Picture of a man's head] ARE HERE PROVIDED WITH / GREEN CROWNS. ALL WHO HAVE BEEN / DRAGGED THROUGH THE COWLED / FLAME OF THIS WORLD, ARE HERE / CLOTHED IN THE BRIGHT RAIMENT OF / THE TEMPEST. HERE ALL WHO SOR-ROW / AND ARE WEARY UNDER STRANGE BUR- / DENS—FEARING DEATH, ARE / SEEN TO ENTER THE WHITE / THRONE ROOM OF GOD / [Pictorial device at right of last three lines] [New York: Padell]

1 blank leaf, 6 leaves, 9-117 pp., 2 blank leaves. 22.5 x 14.5 cm. Black linen end-papers. Green cloth with white lettering. White, yellow, and black dust-wrapper with white lettering.

Published in May at $2.50. 2500 copies printed by Ganis and Harris, New York. *On verso of title-leaf:* "Second Printing 1948."

Contents as (a)

A5 THE TEETH OF THE LION 1942

a. *First Edition*

[In, and extending on either end of, a rectangular block, and pitched at a slight angle:] THE TEETH / OF THE LION / [Entirely within a second block, directly under the first, in white lettering:] IN WHITE SAVAGE CAPS MAKE A / BLOODY PASTURAGE WHERE I AM / LAID DOWN BREAK TEAR KILL IN A / WORLD OF CHEATS DEFILERS RATS / IN PINE WALLS THROUGH THE BLACK / CAMPS WHERE MURDER LIFTS ITS / TEACHING BUT THE GIRLS BY THE / LAKE AND THE GREEN QUICK LAUGH- / ING KIDS IN THE SCHOOLYARD AND / THE SAD WISE BEAUTIFUL GEN-TLE / CLEAN STRONG GOOD LOVING JOYS AS / I AM MADE AND YOU WILL KNOW ME / [In, and extending on either side of, a third rectangular block, pitched at the same angle as the title:] KENNETH / PATCHEN / [Directly beneath the blocks, flush with their left side:] THE POET OF THE MONTH / NEW DIRECTIONS / NORFOLK / CT.

2 leaves [31] pp., 1 leaf. 22.5 x 14 cm. Buff, orange, and green paper-covered boards with white, green, and orange lettering.

Published in October at $1.00; 500 copies printed. *Colophon*: "This Edition of THE TEETH OF THE LION was designed by the author in collaboration with William Candlewood and printed in October MCMXLII with Memphis and Bodoni types at the George Grady Press in New York City."

Contents: The Horses of Yilderin—Legend, For a Little Child—The King of Cold—Turner—The Reason for Skylarks—Midnight Special—Hell Gate Bridge—Timber Wolf—Kibali-Ituri—Moon Sun Sleep—A Theory of Nato-Geography as Advanced By the Tiaphidian Man. . .—Rejecting the Peaceful Overtures of the Kerserians—The Origin of Baseball—The Grand Palace of Versailles—News of a Kind—'Under the Green Ledge'—Polly—Cleveland, Oh—O My Love the Pretty Towns—'Who Holds a Throned Country'—The Lions of Fire Shall Have Their Hunting

b. *First Paperback Edition*

As (a). Simultaneous printing. Printed self-wrappers in same design. Published in October at 50¢; 2500 copies printed.

Contents as (a)

A6   CLOTH OF THE TEMPEST   1943

a. *First Edition*

CLOTH OF / THE TEMPEST / BY KENNETH PATCHEN / [Device] / HARPER & BROTHERS PUBLISHERS / NEW YORK LONDON

1 blank leaf, 4 leaves, 185 pp., 4 leaves. Contents on lining pages front and rear. 24 x 17 cm. Black cloth with white lettering. White dust-wrapper with black lettering.

Published in September at $2.75; 2000 copies printed. *On verso of title-leaf:* "First Edition."

Contents: After A Rondel By Timberlake—'Ah God, Dear Brother, The Mild And Frowning Rose'—All This Is Murder—An Average Entertainment— 'And By Finding This One Earth'—'And The Angel Said'—. . . And When Freedom Is Achieved—Anna Karenina And The Love-Sick River—Anubia— 'Attempt it in Fear'—'At The Cave'—At The Gates Of The Lucky Town— Attila—'Be Music, Night'—'Bring The Womb Its Mother'—But The Arms Never Do—Carnival Late At Night—Chatter—Childhood—Choice Of Forms—'Cloud Drone Boot Rattle'—Cool Brows Quake Not—Coronation Of The Proudest King—Cruelties Of The Sportive Power—Death And Luda As Contending—Decision Of The Beautiful—Definition Of The Mystery— Depafeliusmowkitbeynakildeo—Description Of The Heavens—Discovery Of A New God—'Dreary The Hour, The Path To Splendor'—Easy Rider— Ecstasy Of The Pure—Egypt—'Enjoyment Of Women'—'Fill The Mountain'— Flourish In Thy Season—For The Graduating Class At Harvard—For The Mother Of My Mother's Mother—For Uncle Pritchard—'For Whose Adorn- ment'—Gautama In The Deer Park At Benares—Have You Killed Your Man For Today?—'He Feeds On All'—Help Yourself To Summer—'Hold Thy Tongue, Death!'—How Old The World Is!— 'How Silent Are The Things Of Heaven'—How To Be An Army—In—India—'In Horror The God-Thrown Lie'—'In Shadings Of An Obscure Punishment'—Instructions For Angels— Intensity Of The Forest—'In Thy Falling Have Flame'—Investigation Of Certain Interesting Questions—I Sent A Mental To My Love—'Is It Not Darling Death'—It Is Fully Practical To Create—It Was A Bomby Evening— Jesus Of Nazareth—Lao Tsze—Last Years Of The Poet Khiali—Lips Of The Angel—Lives Of The Swan—Locket—Loves Of The Tragic Owl—Lunch- wagon On Highway 57—Making—Making—Making—Making—May I Ask You A Question, Mr. Youngstown Sheet & Tube?—'Measure The Kings'— Merchant Of Orchards—Mirru—Mohammed—Monster On A Yellow Morn- ing—My Coat Is Dirty—Nainda—Near The River—Nebisinarenellitu—'No Honor May Be Had'—None Shall Stay The White Speech Of His Wandering— Not To Disturb This Gay Gathering—November In Ohio—Now I Went To

The Ringside—'O Fiery River'—O Fill Your Sack With Tiger Cubs—'Of The Same Beauty Were Stars Made'—'O My Darling Troubles Heaven With Her Loveliness'—'Operation Of The Human Being'—'O Terrible Is The Highest Thing'—O That Jesus Boy-What A Grim Lad—'O Ye Wild Sky'—Pleasures Of This Gentle Day—Poem In The House Of The Flame—Progress To A View Of Life—Prometheus Rebound—Ragamuffin Playing With A Really Pretty Creature—'Rest, Heart Of The Tired World'—Rogololisendurikahrium— Sadness Of The Highest Being—Saying On A Gray Field—Scratch A Rich Man And He'll Bleed You—'Seasoning For Adventure'—'She Is The Prettiest Of Creatures'—'She Knows It's Raining—Something Watches You—Speculation On a Rainy Day—Spirit And Blade Of The Highest Truth—Statecraft— Sustainer Of Clay Blessings—Thanksgiving—The Abandoned Forest—The Age Of Pericles—The Ancestral Creature—'The Ancient Whim Of Man's Will'—'The Animal I Wanted'—The Appian Way—The Authority Of Krajova—The Battle Of (   )—The Battle Issus—The Billion Freedoms—The Buffalo That Went To Live At The Waldorf Astoria—The Carriage—'The Carts Of The Wee Blind Lass'—The Castle Of Dealekori—The Caul, Music Of The Snow—The Childhood Of God—The Circle Of Apparent Fates—The Colony Of The Sun—The Continual Ministry Of Thy Anger—The Creation— The Creation Of Africa—The Culture Of The Mislaid People—The Death Of Moby Dick—The Destruction Of Carthage—The Dimensions Of The Morning—"The Dogs Of The Sky'—The Education Of The Waters—The Empire Of Persia—The Enchanted Meadow—The Existence Of Perfection— The Eyes Of Crabs Hold Kingdoms—The Famous Wemezetta Zoo—The First Crusades—'The Flowers Are Born In Shining Wombs'—The Friend Of Heaven—'The Furious Crown Conceals Its Throne'—The Great Questions Operate On All Levels Everywhere—'The Home Of My Spirit'—The House Of The Sleeping Eye—The Impatient Explorer—The Impuissant Surrender To The Name—The Knowledge Of Old Towns—The Lively Enchanters—The Man With The Golden Adam's Apple—The Meeting Of The Roses And The Blind Angel—The Minstrel With The Cloven Hoof—'The Mule Of Water'— The Murder Of Two Men—The Nervousnesses Of Memory—The Poon-Ril Poem—The Prize—The Rean—The Riches Of The Gentlest Prince—'These Are My Great Ones'—The Serpent Is Beginning To Sing—The Shape Of One Enterprise—The Shapes And Intensities Of This Man, This Confucius—The Slums—'The Snow Is On The Ground'—'The Stars Are Occupied'—The Supreme Court Of The United States—The Temple of Diana—The Tribes Of Rakala—The Unfulfilling Brightnesses—The Unnatural History of Peru— 'They Die. The Labors Of God'— Thinking Rock—This Poor life—To a Certain Section Of Our Population—To Enlighten Gnashville, Tennessee—To Say If You Love Someone—To The German People—Trial Of The Chill Giant—Tribute To The Flowers And The Towns—Upon Being Told By A Pretty Girl—Vision Of The Exact Grace—Vita Triumphatrix—'We Followed Her To the Wood'— 'What Gives The River River'—What Is The Beautiful?— 'What Name, Light?'—When The Beautiful Wakes—'When The Stones Burst Into Flame'—When Will The Water Come In?—Where Two O'Clock Came From—While The Panther Sleeps—Who Sees The Fool Sees Through The Fire—Wonderfully Life O Wonderfully Living Heart—Work For Mountains

Note: This book introduced Patchen's "poems-in-drawings" technique.

b. *Second Edition* (1948)

CLOTH OF THE / TEMPEST / KENNETH / PATCHEN [New York: Padell]

> Published in March at $2.50; 2500 copies printed by Ganis and Harris, New York. *On verso of title-leaf:* "This, the second edition, consists of 2500 copies."
>
> *Contents:* As (a), but adds a new poem, "White Lions of Snow," in Patchen's holograph in the front section, beginning on the verso of the dedication leaf, and continuing for three pages.
>
> *Note:* The following, none of which were ever published, were listed as awaiting publication: *I Wonder What Ever Became of Human Beings, The Human Winter, The Surrender of the World, Angel & Monster, The Story of Jeremiah Dork and the Kiladian Forest,* and *Inscriptions For the Dark Rooms of This World.*

A7   MEMOIRS OF A SHY PORNOGRAPHER   1945

a. *First Edition, first impression*

[In black:] THE MEMOIRS / OF A SHY PORNOGRAPHER / [In red:] What I Came From & The Doors Of The / World Are Opened To Me & The First Par- / ty I Ever Went To & The First Real Home / I Ever Had & My Life As A Private Investi- / gator & The Last Party I Ever Went To & / The Story Of My Love & Does The Famous / Detective Know That Love In A Mist / Is Only The Great White Whale Going / Down For The full Count In That Old / Seventh Round & The Deer Are Entering / This Beautiful Forest & The Greatest / And Most Wonderful Plan On Earth / & The House Of The Frowning Heart / & A Radiant Temple Stands Above / The Waters & What Became Of Me / [In black:] AN AMUSEMENT BY / KENNETH PATCHEN / A NEW DIREC-TIONS BOOK

> 242 pp. 22.5 x 14.5 cm. Grey-green paper. Black cloth with gold lettering. Purple dust-wrapper with black and white design and lettering. Spine measures 2.25 cm. across.
>
> Published on September 14 at $3.00. 1800 copies printed.

b. *First Edition, second impression* (1946)

> Title-leaf as (a), but all lettering in black.

242 pp. 22.5 x 14.5 cm. White paper, thinner than (a), spine measuring 1.5 cm. across. Blue cloth with gold lettering. Red dust-wrapper with black and white design and lettering.

Published in January 1946. 3200 copies printed.

c. *First British Edition* (1948)

THE MEMOIRS OF / A SHY PORNOGRAPHER / [Rule] / What I Came From & The Doors Of The World Are / Opened To Me & The First Party I Ever Went To & The / First Real Home I Ever Had & My Life As A Private / Investigator & The Last Party I Ever Went To & The / Story Of My Love & Does The Famous Detective Know / That Love In A Mist Is Only The Great White Whale / Going Down For The Full Count In That Old Seventh / Round & The Deer Are Entering This Beautiful Forest & / The Greatest And Most Wonderful Plan On Earth & The / House Of The Frowning Heart & A Radiant Temple / Stands Above The Waters & What Became Of Me / [Rule] / AN AMUSEMENT BY KENNETH / PATCHEN G.W.P. [London: Grey Walls Press]

236 pp. 17.5 x 12 cm. Grey cloth with black lettering. Tan, blue, grey, and black dust-wrapper with white, blue and black lettering.

d. *First Paperback Edition, first issue* (1958)

THE MEMOIRS OF / A SHY PORNOGRAPHER / [Rule] / What I Came From & The Doors Of The World Are / Opened To Me & The First Party I Ever Went To & The / First Real Home I Ever Had & My Life As A Private / Investigator & The Last Party I Ever Went To & The / Story Of My Love & Does The Famous Detective Know / That Love In A Mist Is Only The Great White Whale / Going Down For The Full Count In That Old Seventh / Round & The Deer Are Entering This Beautiful Forest & / The Greatest And Most Wonderful Plan On Earth & The / House Of Frowning Heart & A Radiant Temple / Stands Above The Waters & What Became Of Me / [Rule] / AN AMUSEMENT by KEN-NETH PATCHEN / CITY LIGHTS BOOKS / San Francisco

235 [1] pp. 16.5 x 11.5 cm. Grey and black stiff paper with white lettering. Cover by Ray Johnson. Later issues identified as such as the bottom of the back cover.

Published in February at $1.75. 6000 copies printed.

e. *Italian Edition* (1962)

Memorie Di Un Pornografo Timido. Milano: Sugar Editore, 1962. Trans. Katharina Behrens.

f. *German Edition* (1964)

Erinnerungen Eines Schuchternen Pornografen. Wiesbaden: Limes Verlag, 1964. Trans. Luciano Bianciardi.

g. *Second Paperback Edition* (1965)

As (b), but reduced in size [20 x 13.5 cm.] and in stiff paper wrappers. *On verso of title-leaf:* "First Paperback printing." To date four printings of 5000. Later printings identified as such on verso of title-leaf.

h. *Danish Edition* (1968)

Af En Bly Pornografs Memoirer. Kobenhaven: Stig Vendelkaers, 1968. Trans. Tania Orum and Hans-Jorgen Neilson.

A8   AN ASTONISHED EYE LOOKS   ([1945] 1946)
                              OUT OF THE AIR
a. *First Edition, first impression*

[White lettering on screened beige:] AN AST / ONISH / ED EYE / LOOKS / OUT OF / THE AIR / [Superimposed on previous:] KENNETH / PATCHEN / FOR MIRIAM / UNTIDE PRESS: WALDPORT: OREGON [Facing page in red lettering:] AN AST / ONISH / ED EYE / LOOKS / OUT OF / THE AIR /

4 leaves [35] pp., 1 leaf. 24 x 17 cm. Heavy black paper; slick white label wrapped around fold, extending 14 cm. onto front and back covers, and carrying the title [in black] and author [in red] on each. Each page carries the title in light letters as it appears on the title-leaf.

Printed on December 31, 1945; none offered for sale. [1800] printed. Miriam Patchen writes, "Of the first press-run of some eighteen hundred impressions less than fifty copies [actually about thirty] survived a mechanical accident which made necessary a new printing; twenty-three of these "good" copies came into possession of the author, who then signed and numbered eleven of them as a record." These copies, which vary in the darkness of impression, all bear a red paper inserted by Patchen, describing the book, and numbered and signed by him.

Colophon: "AN ASTONISHED EYE LOOKS OUT OF THE AIR was designed by Kemper Nomland, Jr. from a suggestion of the author. It is hand set in Futura types in an edition of 1,950 copies. The tint-block was printed by The Franklin Press, Corvallis, Oregon." On verso of the *title-leaf:* "From *Before the Brave,* 1936: poems 5 and 15. From *First Will & Testament,* 1939; poems 4, 9 and 16. From *The Dark Kingdom,* 1942; poems 3, 8, 11, 25 and 30. From *The Teeth of the Lion,* 1942: poems 6 and 27. From *Cloth of the Tempest,* 1943: poems 2, 10, 14, 18, 19, 26, 31 and 33. Appearing for the first time: poems 1, 7, 12, 13, 17, 20, 21, 22, 23, 24, 28, 29, 32 and 34."

Contents: 1. 'The Stars Go To Sleep So Peacefully'—2. The Dimensions Of The Morning—3. The Wolf of Winter—4. The State Of The Nation—5. A Letter To The Young Men—6. The Origin Of Baseball—7. The Monster And The Angel—8. Irkalla's White Caves—9. Do The Dead Know What Time It is?— 10. 'O Fiery River'—11. The Climate Of War—12. The Dazzling Burden— 13. 'I Always Return To This Place'—14. 'Keep Life'—15. Let Us Have Madness Openly—16. The Fox—17. Landscape Of The Uneasy Soul—18. The Battle Of (   )—19. Instruction For Angels—20. 'Beings So Hideous That The Air Weeps Blood'—21. Summer Day—22. I Feel Drunk All The Time— 23. Science Talked To—24. 'Joined Together By The Rule Of Peaceful Love'— 25. The Naked Land—26. The Billion Freedoms—27. The Lions Of Fire Shall Have Their Hunting—28. 'Poems Which Are Written By The Soul'—29. At The Entrance To The Other World—30. These Unreturning Destinies— 31. 'How Silent Are The Things Of Heaven'—32. Credit To Paradise—33. What Is The Beautiful?—34. 'The Way Men Live Is A Lie'

Notes: The book was printed in a conscientous objectors' camp after regular work hours. *Kenneth Patchen: A First Bibliography* [see Miscellanea 6] by Gail Eaton [Miriam Patchen] was sometimes taped into the front of it.

b. *First Edition, second impression* (1946)

As (a), but without the hand-written limitation notice. 1,950 copies printed at 35¢.

A9   OUTLAW OF THE LOWEST PLANET   1946

First Edition

KENNETH PATCHEN / OUTLAW / OF THE   / LOWEST PLANET /   SELECTED AND INTRODUCED BY / DAVID GASCOYNE / WITH A PREFACE BY / ALEX COMFORT / LONDON / THE GREY WALLS PRESS

1 blank leaf, 2 leaves, v-xviii, 83 pp., 2 blank leaves. 23.75 x 14 cm. Black cloth with gold lettering. Light blue dust-wrapper with blue and red lettering.

Publication date and number of copies unknown. 8s 6d. *On verso of title-leaf:* "First published 1946."

Contents: Preface by Alex Comfort—"Introducing Kenneth Patchen" By David Gascoyne—From 'First Will & Testament' (1939): Behold One Of Several Little Christs—The Hangman's Great Hands—And What With The Blunders, What With The Real Humour Of The Address—Boxers Hit Harder When Women Are Around—A Revolutionary Prayer—All The Bright Foam Of Talk—Street Corner College—Fifth Dimension—Can The Harp Shoot Through Its Propellers?—Niobe—Heine Lived In Germany—Nice Day For A Lynching—Elegy For The Silent Voices And The Joiners Of Everything—Eve Of St. Agony Or The Middleclass Was Sitting On Its Fat—Three Early Poems: (1) The Sea Has Caves And Urns (2) Geography of Music (3) At The New Year—The Overworld—All That Night Lights Were Seen Moving In Every Direction, And Voices Heard—In Judgement Of The Leaf—'These Have Gone With Silent Hands, Seeking'—From The Argument To The Hunted City, I-VII—From 'The Dark Kingdom' (1942): The Rites Of Darkness—The Second People—Cloth Of The Tempest—The Village Tudda—Irkalla's White Caves—These Unreturning Destinies—The Manifold Fusions—The Crowded Net—The Meaning Of Life—Continuation Of The Landscape—How God Was Made—Lenada—Canticle Of Pilkes Ludd—Oniiasy—Pastoral—Saturday Night In The Parthenon—Outlaw Of The Lowest Planet—The Climate Of War—There Is One Who Watches—From 'The Teech of the Lion' (1942): Turner—The Origin Of Baseball—The Grand Palace Of Versailles—'Under The Green Ledge'—The Lions Of Fire Shall Have Their Hunting—From 'Cloth of the Tempest' (1943): Cruelties Of The Sportive Power—The Age Of Pericles—The Billion Freedoms—Pleasures Of This Gentle Day—'When The Stones Burst Into Flame'—Where Two O'Clock Came From—Intensity Of The Forest—Investigation Of Certain Interesting Questions—The Carts Of The Wee Blind Lass—'Ah God, Dear Brother, The Mild And Frowning Rose' —The Knowledge Of Old Towns—My Coat Is Dirty—For The Mother Of My Mother's Mother—O Fill Your Sack With Tiger Cubs—Lives Of The Swan—The Serpent Is Beginning To Sing On The Doorsetp Of Your World— The Tribes Of Rakala—The Continual Ministry Of Thy Anger—'O Fiery River'—The Caul, Music Of The Snow . . .—'Rest, Heart Of The Tired World'

A10   THE SELECTED POEMS   1946
OF KENNETH PATCHEN

a. *First Edition*

THE / SELECTED POEMS / OF / KENNETH PATCHEN /
The New Classics / A NEW DIRECTIONS BOOK

1 blank leaf, x, 86 pp., 1 blank leaf. 18.5 x 12.5 cm. Tan cloth with red lettering. Red and white dust-wrapper with black lettering.

Published December 2 at $1.50. 2000 copies printed by the Vail Ballou Press, Binghampton, New York. Jacket design by Albert Lustig. *On verso of Dedication leaf:* "The poems in this selection are taken from the following volumes and

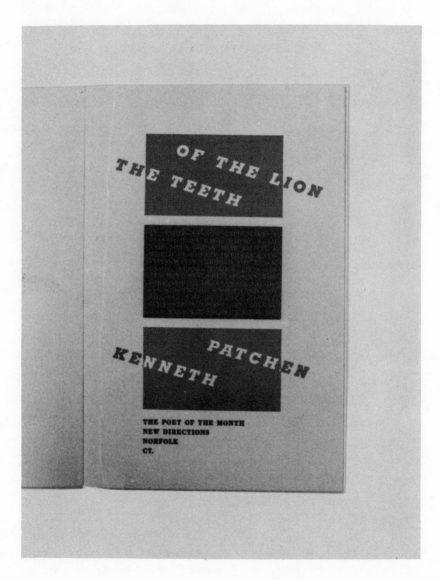

Title Page of *The Teeth of the Lion* (1942). A5a.

Title Pages of *An Astonished Eye Looks Out of the Air* (1946). A8b.

were chosen by the publisher, not the author. The provenance of each poem is listed in the table of contents by number."

1. *Before The Brave* (1936); 2. *First Will & Testament* (1939); 3. *The Dark Kingdom* (1941); 4. *The Teeth Of The Lion* (1942); 5. *Cloth Of The Tempest* (1943); 6. *An Astonished Eve Looks Out Of The Air* (1945).

Contents: As She Was Thus Alone in the Clear Moonlight (2)—And What With The Blunders (2)—These Unreturning Destinies (3)—Let Us Have Madness (1)—We Leave You Pleasure (1)—Do The Dead Know What Time It Is? (2)— 'The Snow Is Deep on the Ground' (5)—The Reason For Skylarks (4)—She Knows It's Raining (5)—I Feel Drunk All The Time (6)—I Don't Want to Startle You (2)—The Rites Of Darkness (3)—'O Fiery River' (5)—The Origin of Baseball (4)—The Grand Palace of Versailles (4)—Irkalla's White Caves (3)— We Must Be Slow (1)—The Wolf of Winter (3)—The Billion Freedoms (5)— Fall of the Evening Star (2)—The Fox (2)—Instructions for Angels (5)—A Temple (3)—She Had Concealed Him in a Deep Dark Dave (2)—The Hangman's Great Hands (2)—The Forms of Knowledge (3)—The Stars Go to Sleep so Peacefully (6)—The Character of Love Seen as a Search for the Lost (2)— Continuation of the Landscape (3)—'For Losing Her Love All Would I profane' (3)—'As We Ar so Wonderfully Done . . .' (3)—He Was Alone (as in Reality) . . . (2)—My Generation Reading the Newspapers (1)—For the Mother of My Mother's Mother (5)—Behold, One of Several Little Christs (2)—Written After Reading an Item in the Paper About a Young Lady Who Went Mad upon Forsaking Her Lover. He Is Here Assumed to Speak (3)—'For Whose Adornment' (5)—'Of The Same Beauty Were Stars Made' (5)—To a Certain Section of Our Population (5)—May I Ask You a Question, Mr. Youngstown Sheet & Tube? (5)—The Climate of War (3)—The Impatient Explorer (5)—Street Corner College (2)—Credit to Paradise (6)—Birthday Greetings for W.C.(hurchill) and His Pals (6)—The Figure Motioned with Its Mangled Hand Towards the Wall Behind It (2)—Avarice and Ambition Only Were the First Builders of Towns and Founders of Empire (2)—'Be Music, Night' (5)—What Is the Beautiful? (5)—The Dimensions of the Morning (5)—"And When Freedom Is Achieved . . . " (5)—The Unfulfilling Brightnesses (5)—Mohammed (5)—How to Be an Army (5)—Gautama in the Deer Park at Benares (5)—The Man with the Golden Adam's Apple (5)—'O My Darling Troubles Heaven . . .' (5)—The Lions of Fire Shall Have Their Hunting (4)—A Vision for the People of America (new).

b. *Enlarged Edition* (1957)

THE / SELECTED POEMS / OF / KENNETH PATCHEN / ENLARGED EDITION / The New Classics / A NEW DIRECTIONS BOOK

xii, 146 pp. 19 x 13 cm. White cloth with red lettering. White and red dustwrapper with black lettering.

Published February 14 at $2.00. 2000 copies printed by Vail-Ballou Press, Binghamton, New York. *On verso of dedication-leaf:* "The poems in this selection are taken from the following volumes and were chosen by the publisher, not the author. The provenance of each poem is listed in the table of contents by number." 1. *Before The Brave* (1936), 2. *First Will & Testament* (1939), 3. *The Dark Kingdom* (1942), 4. *The Teeth Of The Lion* (1942), 5. *Cloth Of The Tempest* (1943), 6. *An Astonished Eye Looks Out Of The Air* (1945), 7. *Red Wine And Yellow Hair* (1949), 8. *When We Were Here Together* (1952-1957), 9. *The Famous Boating Party* (1954), 10. *Hurrah For Anything* (1957).

Contents: As She Was Thus Alone in the Clear Moonlight (2)—And What with the Blunders (2)—These Unreturning Destinies (3)—Let Us Have Madness (1)—We Leave You Pleasure (1)—Do the Dead Know What Time It Is? (2)— 'The Snow Is Deep on the Ground' (5)—The Reason for Skylarks (4)—She Knows It's Raining (5)—I Feel Drunk All the Time (6)—I Don't Want to Startle You (2)—The Rites of Darkness (3)—'O Fiery River' (5)—The Origin of Baseball (4)—The Grand Palace of Versailles (4)—Irkalla's White Caves (3)—We Must Be Slow (1)—The Wolf of Winter (3)—The Billion Freedoms (5)—Fall of the Evening Star (2)—The Fox (2)—Instructions for Angels (5)—A Temple (3) —She Had Concealed Him in a Deep Dark Cave (2)—The Hangman's Great Hands (2)—The Forms of Knowledge (3)—The Stars Go to Sleep so Peacefully (6)—The Character of Love Seen as a Search for the Lost (2)—Continuation of the Landscape (3)—'For Losing Her Love All Would I Profane' (3)—'As We Are so Wonderfully Done . . .' (3)—He Was Alone (as in Reality) . . . (2)—My Generation Reading the Newspapers (1)—For the Mother of My Mother's Mother (5)—Behold, One of Several Little Christs (2)—Written After Reading an Item in the Paper About a Young Lady Who Went Mad upon Forsaking Her Lover. He Is Here Assumed to Speak (3)—'For Whose Adornment' (5)—'Of the Same Beauty Were Stars Made' (5)—To a Certain Section of Our Population (5)—May I Ask You a Question, Mr. Youngstown Sheet & Tube? (5)—The Climate of War (3)—The Impatient Explorer (5)—Street Corner College (2)— Credit to paradise (6)— Birthday Greetings for W.C(hurchill) and His Pals (6) —The Cloth of the Tempest (3)—Have You Killed Your Man for Today? (5)— Nice Day for a Lynching (2)—Fog (2)—23rd Street Runs into Heaven (2)— There Is One Who Watches (3)—Can the Harp Shoot Through Its Propellers? (2)—Eve of St. Agony or The Middleclass Was Sitting on Its Fat (2)—'There Is Nothing False in Thee' (3)—'Rest, Heart of the Tired World' (5)—How God Was Made (3)—Pastoral (3)—Now I Went Down to the Ringside and Little Henry Armstrong Was There (5)—Boxers Hit Harder When Women Are Around (2)—The Poor Child with the Hooked Hands (2)—Death Will Amuse Them (2)—In Memory of Kathleen (2)—The Deer and the Snake (2)—Religion Is That I Love You (2)—The Soldier and the Star (2)—The State of the Nation (2)—All the Bright Foam of Talk (2)—But the Images of His Former Dreams . . . (2)—The Figure Motioned with Its Mangled Hand Towards the Wall Behind It (2)—Avarice and Ambition Only Were the First Builders of Towns and Founders of Empire (2)—'Be Music, Night' (5)—What Is the Beautiful? (5)— The Dimensions of the Morning (5)—"And When Freedom Is Achieved . . ." (5)—The Unfulfilling Brightnesses (5)—Mohammed (5)—How to Be an Army (5)—Gautama in the Deer Park at Benares (5)—The Man with the Golden Adam's Apple (5)—'O My Darling Troubles Heaven . . .' (5)—The Lions of Fire Shall Have Their Hunting (4)—A Vision for the People of America (new)—The Murder of Two Men by a Young Kid Wearing Lemon-colored Gloves (5)—Red Wine and Yellow Hair (7)—The New Being (7)—A Plate of Steaming Fish (7)— The Lute in the Attic (7)—The Orange Bears (7)—If a Poem Can Be Headed into Its Proper Current (7)—'Do Me That Love' (7)—Fog Over the Sea and the Sun Going Down (7)—A Pile of Rusty Beer Cans (7)—Poor Gorrel (7)—For Miriam (8)—Lonesome Boy Blues (8)—But of Life? (8)—The Unanswering Correspondences (8)—Limpidity of Silences (8)—So Be It (8)—The Everlasting Contenders (8)—What Splendid Birthdays (8)—Always Another Viewpoint (8) —A Trueblue Gentleman (8)—Where Every Prospect (8)—The Constant Bridegrooms (8)—The Unreturning Hosts (8)—Folly of Clowns (8)—All the Flowery (8)—Lowellville Cemetery: Twilight (8)—Little Cannibal's Bedtimesong (8)— Encounter at Nightfall (8)—In Order To (9)—Soon It Will (9)—There Are Two (9)—Opening the Window (9)—It Takes Few Kinds (9)—To Be Charmed (9)— Moon "Continued" (9)—The Great Sledmakers (9)—Not Many Kingdoms Left (9)—Often Was It (9)—The Cowboy Who Went to College (10)—The Little Man with Wooden Hair (10)—The Tame Streetcar Conductor (10)—The Careless Little Spy (10)—The Forgetful Little Commuter (10)—The Man Who Was Shorter Than Himself (10)—The Little Man Who Saw A Grass (10)—The Celery-Flute Player (10)—I Went to the City (10)—One Who Hopes (10)— Only Cherries? (10)—All the Roary Night (10)—How come? (10)—The Peaceful Lier (10—And with the Sorrows of This Joyousness (10)

c. *First Paperback Edition* (1964)

Selected Poems / By / Kenneth Patchen / A New Directions Paperbook

Pagination and size as (b) Stiff paper wraps; photo of Patchen on cover.

Published in April at $1.75. 6000 copies printed by the Vail-Ballou Press, Binghamton, New York. Later printings identified as such on verso of title-leaf.

Contents as (b)

All   SLEEPERS AWAKE   1946

a. *First Edition, special issue (white)*

[Title page consists of two facing pages. First, black and yellow lettering:] KENNETH / PATCHEN / [Second, yellow and red lettering:] SLEEPERS / AWAKE [New York: Padell]

389 pp. 23.5 x 16 cm. White Buckram with gold lettering on spine. Individual watercolors painted by Patchen pasted onto each cover. Numbered and signed.

Published in December at $10.00. 75 copies printed by John Felsberg, New York.

b. *First Edition, special issue (red)*

Title page, pagination, size as (a).

Red Buckram with gold lettering on spine. Numbered and signed.

Published in December at $5.00. 73 copies printed by John Felsberg, New York.

c. *First Edition, regular issue*

Pagination, size as (a). Title page as (a) but only black and rd lettering.

Grey cloth with gold lettering on spine. Black and White dust-wrapper with black, white, and red lettering.

Published in December at $3.50. 3500 copies printed by John Felsberg, New York.

d. *First Paperback Edition* (1969)

Title page as (a), except all lettering in black.

382 pp. 20 x 13.5 cm. Stiff printed wrappers.

Published on October 15. 3500 copies printed; to date two additional printings of 3500. *On verso of title-leaf:* "First published as ND Paperbook 286 in 1969." Cover design by the author. Later printings identified as such on verso of title-leaf and upper right corner of back cover.

e. *First German Edition* (1963)

Berlin-Wilmersdorf: Gebhardt Verlag, 1963.

f. *Second German Edition* (1970)

Frankfurt: Marz Verlag, 1970.

A12   PANELS FOR THE WALLS OF HEAVEN   1946

a. *First Edition, regular issue*

[Along right margin:] K / E / N / N / E / T / H / P / A / T / C / H / E / N [Centered:] PANELS FOR THE WALLS / OF HEAVEN / BERN / PORTER / 1946

1 blank leaf, 1 leaf, 67 pp., 2 blank leaves. 20.5 x 20.5 cm. Raw boards with black and red lettering. Yellow-brown dust-wrapper with red and black lettering.

Published at $4.50. 750 copies printed by the Gillick Press, Berkeley, California.

Contents: Panels One through Forty-four

Note: Porter writes, "[Patchen] positively did not like color of ink used, shape of book, size of book, linen effect of paper; did not see proofs, threatened to sue me if words For Miriam were not used and then threatened to sue me generally . . . Refused to aid the book sales in any way and was my total enemy for years . . . The book sold at the time for $4.50 and had few sales and hence [was] a publishing loss of major proportions . . ."

b. *First Edition, special (painted) issue*

Title-leaf, pagination, and size as (a).

Thick, raw boards, each bearing a cover individually painted by the author. Numbered and signed on back cover, and covered with an acetate jacket.

150 copies prepared in this manner. The raw copies were Patchen's royalty, and he sold the finished "painted books" for $8.50

A13 PICTURES OF LIFE AND OF DEATH 1946

First Edition

[In black:] PICTURES / [In red:] OF LIFE [In black:] AND / OF DEATH / [In red:] KENNETH / PATCHEN [New York: Padell]

7-32 pp. 23.5 x 15.5 cm. Pictorial self-wraps, cover reading "26 poems / pic-1 / kenneth patchen," with a drawing of two figures in red, white, and black, and white and black lettering.

Published December 1946 at $1.00; 2500 copies printed. *On verso of title-leaf:* "First Edition." *On verso of dedication-leaf:* "Two Thousand Five Hundred Copies Of This First Edition Of Pictures Of Life And Of Death, Set In Caslon Old Face, Greco & Others, Have Been Printed On Tweedweave Laid Paper. Designed By The Author & Publication Completed December, Nineteen Hundred & Forty Six By John Felsberg, Inc., New York. None of these poems has appeared in print before."

Contents: So It Ends—'I'd Want Her Eyes To Fill With Wonder.'—The Valley-Sleeper, The Children, The Snakes, And The Giant.—Of All The Years Since The World Began, 1927 Is The Farthest Off Of All.—Winter Poem—Notes For The Death Of The World—Shadows And Spring Flowers—Drenched With Color And Sound—O All Down Within The Pretty Meadow—About The

Only Thing Beautiful The Snow Does Is Snow—'Pretty Glow On The Water'—
History In A Minor Key—'Where Some Beast Has Torn The Grass'—All The
Roses Of The World—Don't Wash Your Hair In The Streetcar, Nora Dear—
But I Don't Know—naked girls/are bathing—It Is Early Evening—Who Asked
For A Poem—Yellow Stones—Vinegar And Perfume—Fun In The Golden
Voice—'O Sleeping Lay The Maiden Snow'—The Throne That Rides The
Water—Land Of The Never-Ending Heart—'Christ! Christ! Christ! That
The World'

A14   THEY KEEP RIDING DOWN   [1946-7]
                         ALL THE TIME

First Edition

[Arranged in an oval shape, the title going down each side] [In
black:] KENNETH / [In red:] THEY THEY / KEEP KEEP /
RIDING RIDING / DOWN / ALL ALL / THE THE / TIME
TIME / [In black:] PATCHEN [New York: Padell]

> 6-32 pp. 24 x 16 cm. Plain paper with half-title, printed white stiff paper self-
> wraps with red, grey, and black lettering and decoration.

> Published in January 1947 [Copyright 1946] at $1.00. 2500 copies printed.
> Designed and with a cover illustration by the author.

A15   CCCLXXIV POEMS   [1947-8]

First Edition

No title-page. [New York: Padell]

> Binding-together of the Padell reprints of *First Will and Testament, The Dark
> Kingdom,* and *Cloth of the Tempest.* Black linen with flat back; gold lettering
> on spine. Jacket [made by Miriam Patchen] of heavy leather grain blue paper
> with a two-inch square cut out to expose spine lettering and strip with title [cut
> from mailing piece] on front.

> Printed at same time as trade copies. 126 copies. Sold by Patchen at Old Lyme,
> Conn. for $6.00. *Colophon:* [inside front cover] "CCCLXXIV POEMS is made
> up of the complete texts of *First Will and Testament, The Dark Kingdom* and
> *Cloth of the Tempest,* which have been brought together under this single cover
> in an edition of only 126 copies . . . printed on Rag Laid paper, specially bound,
> stamped in genuine gold, numbered and signed by the Author."

> *Contents:* Entire contents of three previous books—*First Will and Testament,
> The Dark Kingdom,* and *Cloth of the Tempest.*

A16   SEE YOU IN THE MORNING   [1947] 1948

a. *First Edition*

KENNETH PATCHEN / See You In / The Morning / [Device: Drawing of a tree] / PADELL NEW YORK

256 pp. 21 x 14 cm. Blue cloth with gold lettering. Blue and white dust-wrapper with blue, white and purple lettering and decoration.

Published on March 20, 1948 [Copyright 1947] at $2.75. Undetermined number of copies printed by John Felsberg, New York.

Note: This was Patchen's only "conventional" novel, and it was highly successful financially. Though he wrote it to help Padell recoup substantial losses resulting from the publication of *Sleepers Awake* and other books of Patchen's which he had sponsored, Padell himself refused to allow it to become a book club selection as he felt that would compromise Patchen's artistic integrity.

b. *First Edition, reissue*

Identical to (a), except the imprint. Beneath Padell on the title-leaf, the copies stamped WEHMAN BROS. / PUBLISHERS / 158 MAIN STREET / HACKENSACK, N.J. It was apparently a result of part of the edition being remaindered.

c. *First British Edition* (1949)

KENNETH PATCHEN / [Rule] / SEE YOU / IN THE MORNING / [Rule] / GREY WALLS PRESS

232 pp. 19 x 12.5 cm. Tan cloth with black lettering. Black, red, brown, and blue dust-wrapper with white lettering.

Published at 8s. 6d.

d. *French Edition* (1950)

A Demain, Mon Amour. Paris: Gallimard, 1950. Trans. Adeline Arnaud.

e. *Italian Edition* (1950)

Arrivederci A Domani. Torino: Giulio Einaudi, 1950. Trans. Bruno Fonzi.

f. *First Swedish Edition* (1950)

Vi Ses I Morgon Bitti. Stockholm: Hugo Geber, 1950. Trans. Siri Thorngren Olin.

g. *Second Swedish Edition* (1952)

Brev Till Gud Och Andra. Stockholm: Hugo Geber, 1952. Trans. Lars Gustav Hellstrom.

A17   TO SAY IF YOU LOVE SOMEONE   [1948]

a. *First Edition, first state*

[All within rectangular single rule, surrounded by decorative floral border:] TO SAY IF / YOU LOVE / SOMEONE / And Other Selected / Love Poems / by / KENNETH PATCHEN / The Decker Press / Prairie City, Illinois

2 blank leaves, 3 leaves [32] p., 1 blank leaf, 1 leaf, 3 blank leaves. 17 x 12.5 cm. Off-yellow cloth with black lettering within a purple border. Pink and purple dust-wrapper with red and blue lettering. Later green dust-wrapper with black lettering.

Date of printing unknown. Perhaps two hundred in entire edition; about twenty of this first state.

Colophon: "This book has been printed from Fairfield and Bondoni Types on Linweave Text Paper. Design and Typography by James A. Decker."

Contents: For Miriam (Since the tiny yellow rose)—O My Darling Troubles Heaven With Her Loveliness—'O Sleeping Lay The Maiden Snow'—'We Go Out Together Into The Staring Town'—'From My High Love I Look At That Poor World There'—As She Was Thus Alone In The Clear Moonlight—'Be Music, Night'—'She Is the Prettiest of Creatures'—'Wonderfully Life O Wonderfully Living Heart'—Fall Of The Evening Star—Do I Not Deal With Angels —She Had Concealed Him In A Deep Dark Cave—'O My Love The Pretty Towns'—Creation—O My Dearest—The Character Of Love Seen As A Search For The Lost—Religion Is That I Love You—'Where My Stag-Antlered Love Moves'—23rd Street Runs Into Heaven—Five Early Poems—'The Sea Is Awash With Roses'—To Say If You Love Someone—In Judgement Of The Leaf—'As Frothing Wounds of Roses'—'For Losing Her Love All Would I Profane'—'The Snow Is Deep On The Ground'—'As We Are So Wonderfully Done With Each Other'

Notes: Miriam Patchen writes: "All copies are the same as far as the fine print job goes. James Decker used types Kenneth suggested. He was a perfectionist at working with his types and press, it seemed to us . . . *To Say* was completed, and for The Decker Press, quite quickly . . . We received a few copies. Kenneth was very pleased. Not long after, Louis Zukofsky told us that Margery Lattimer, I think, had called him telling him of a radio news broadcast she'd heard. James Decker's car had been found abandoned in Minnesota somewhere. He was missing. A while after that his sister and a New York poet (male) had been found in a car in what appeared to be a case of murder-suicide . . . Several years later we received a letter from state controllers saying that there were some bound copies of [the book]. If [Patchen] wished them, he could have them for a small fee and shipping charges." The Patchens received the books and stored them in their house.

b. *First Edition, first state (special copies)*

As (a). Between 1960 and his death in 1972, Patchen covered some of these with handmade Japanese papers, preparatory to painting. Six were actually painted; they do not bear a limitation notice.

c. *First Edition, second state*

As (a) except hard paper cover with an "all-over" design and pasted on label. No dust-wrapper.

d. *First Edition, third state*

As (a). This was the state planned for general circulation. Cloth boards reproducing an old quilt design with a dust-wrapper of the same design.

A18　　　　　RED WINE AND YELLOW HAIR　　　　　1949

a. *First Edition, regular issue*

KENNETH PATCHEN / RED WINE & / YELLOW HAIR / NEW DIRECTIONS [Black dot] NEW YORK

64 pp. 23.5 x 16 cm. Yellow cloth with red and black lettering. Yellow dust-wrapper with red and black lettering. Design by Gertrude Huston.

Published at $2.00. 2000 copies printed by John Felsberg, New York.

Contents: The Hunter—'White Lions are Roaring on the Water'—A Lost Poem—Hovenweep—Week-end Bathers—The Lute in the Attic—Old Man— If a Poem can be Headed into its Proper Current Someone Will Take It within His Heart to the Power and Beauty of Everybody—The Radiance in a Dark Wood—A Plate of Steaming Fish—'Breathe on the Living'—Portrait of the Artist as an Interior Decorator—The Value of Cautions for This Journey— Summer Storm by the Sea—To Bunneni, Hake, and Clem Maugre, the Seers of Gloccus-as Well as to All Other Forgotten Minstrels of Our Enlightenment— The Orange Bears—Shapes—And a Man Went Out Alone—'O when I Take my Love out Walking'—After an Old Song—The New Being—Wouldn't You Be after a Jaunt of 964,000,000,000,000 Miles?—How Jimsey O'Roon and Peter Stack, Coal Miners, Came to be Put in the Ferbettville (Pa.) Jail Early one

Saturday Night—Poor Gorrel—A Pile of Rusty Beer Cans—Family Portrait—
An Old Pair of Shoes—'Blind'd be the Last of Men'—The Little Black Train—
To the Tune of an Ancient Song—Winter at the Inn—The Event at Konna—
'This Summer Earth'—Down in the Lone Valley—Two for History—Fog over
the Sea and the Sun Going Down—Latesummer Blues—'Do Me that Love'—
Lament for the Makers of Songs—Red Wine and Yellow Hair

b. *First Edition, painted issue*

Title-page, pagination, and contents as (a). Boards extended to 23.5 cm.

Original hand-painted covers. Numbered and signed. 108 copies available
at $7.00.

A 19   IN PEACEABLE CAVES   1950

First Edition

KENNETH PATCHEN / [Rule] / IN / PEACEABLE / CAVES /
a selection of poems / made by Wrey Gardiner / [Rule] / THE
GREY WALLS PRESS

viii, 74 pp. 22 x 14 cm. Yellow cloth

On verso of title-leaf: "First published in England in 1950 by the Grey Walls
Press Limited . . . Printed in Great Britain by The Alcuin Press." Soon after the
book was printed, the warehouse in which the completed books were stored
burned down. It was never reprinted, and the only copy which is known to exist
is one which was sent to Patchen for his inspection just prior to the fire. He
decorated the front and back covers with gold foil and attached a small black
and yellow relief painting to the front. The copy is now at the University of
California at Santa Cruz.

Contents: For Miriam (As frothing wounds of roses)—The Fox—Fall Of The
Evening Star—She Had Concealed Him In A Deep Dark Cave—As She Was
Thus Alone In The Clear Moonlight—The Character Of Love Seen As A
Search For The Lost—But The Images Of His Former Dreams Still Haunted
Him—Religion Is That I Love You—The Deer And The Snake—In Memory
Of Kathleen—23rd Street Runs Into Heaven—The Forms Of Knowledge—A
Devotion—Heaven And Earth—The Naked Land—'We Go Out Together Into
The Staring Town'—'As We Are So Wonderfully Done With Each Other'—
The Wolf Of Winter—Written After Reading . . .—The Reason For Skylarks—
O My Love The Pretty Towns—Mirru—The Battle Of (   )—'O My
Darling Troubles Heaven With Her Loveliness'—'The Snow Is Deep On The
Ground'—Thinking Rock—Have You Killed Your Man For Today?—The
Dimensions Of The Morning—Instructions For Angels—'How Silent Are
The Things Of Heaven'—'I Always Return To This Place'—Let Us Have

Madness Openly—Notes For The Death Of The World—'Christ! Christ! Christ! That The World'—So It Ends—'White Lions Are Roaring On The Water'—A Lost Poem—Hovenweep—Old Man—If A Poem Can Be Headed Into Its Proper Current—The Radiance In A Dark Wood—A Plate Of Steaming Fish—The Value Of Cautions For This Journey—The Orange Bears—'O When I Take My Love Out Walking'—After An Old Song—The New Being—How Jimsey O'Roon And Peter Stack, Coal Miners . . .—The Event At Konna—'This Summer Earth'—Down In The Lone Valley—Two For History—Red Wine And Yellow Hair—Lament For The Makers Of Songs—'Do Me That Love'

A20   ORCHARDS, THRONES, & CARAVANS   1952

a. *First Edition, Engravers Edition*

[In black:] KENNETH PATCHEN / [In blue:] ORCHARDS, THRONES / & CARAVANS / [In black:] THE PRINT WORKSHOP

52 [1] pp. 17.5 x 14.5 cm. Stiff white paper with white self-wraps and gold lettering, with an original engraving on the front cover. Numbered and signed.

Published on June 6 at $15.00. 90 copies printed. *Colophon:* ". . . the Engravers Editions of Orchards, Thrones, & Caravans, consisting of ninety numbered copies signed by engraver and poet featuring a copper engraving by David Ruff / Holland Van Gelder paper / Eric Gill's Perpetua type bound in hand-made Chatham Parchment by Perry G. Davis / hand set and printed at the Greenwood Press work completed June 6th 1952."

Contents: Poems for Miriam (As beautiful as the hands; O green birds; O pure / And fair as the clouds)—But of Life?—The Green Fires—Lowellville Cemetary; Twilight—Watching Neighbors' Children—The Constant Bridegrooms—The Unreturning Hosts—Folly of Clowns—All the FLowery—At Grandmother's Wake—Two Ghosts Together—Where Every Prospect—A Jungle Village—Who Walks There?—So Be It—Under a Tree—In the Moonlight—Beautiful You Are—Day of Rabblement—Should Be Sufficient—My Pretty Animals—Encounter at Nightfall—Little Cannibal's Bedtimesong—The Cruelkind Swans—The Oldest Conversation—Lonesome Boy Blues—It's a Smallworld—The Magical Mouse—A Trueblue Gentleman—An Unexpected Impasse—An Easy Decision—Always Another Viewpoint—The Irate Songster—A Vanishing Institution—Lament and Lullaby—The Unanswering Correspondences—Limpidity of Silences—The Bird-Queen—The Wonderful Sun!—The Everlasting Contenders—What Splendid Birthdays—All is Safe—What There Is

b. *First Edition, Vellum Edition*

Title-leaf, pagination, size as (a).

Binding as (a) but without engraving on cover. 120 copies sold at $8.00. Numbered and signed.

Colophon: ". . . the Vellum Edition of Orchards Thrones and Caravans consisting of one hundred and twenty numbered copies, signed by the poet / hand made Curfew paper / Eric Gill's Perpetua type bound in Invicta parchment by Perry G. Davis / hand set and printed by David Ruff at the Greenwood Press work completed June 6th 1952."

c. *First Edition, variant copies*

Title-leaf and size as (a). Pagination and contents as (a), but no colophon

A number of years after the publication of *Orchards, Thrones & Caravans*, Miriam Patchen took some of the left-over, stitched but unbound sheets from the edition, and bound three copies herself, after excising the colophon. The copies bear Patchen's signature on the title-leaf. None was sold.

A21   FABLES AND OTHER LITTLE TALES   1953

a. *First edition, regular issue*

[Title page consists of two facing pages. First, in yellow:] K [covering most of page] / [Superimposed in black:] FABLES / AND [Below K] JONATHAN WILLIAMS [Black dot] PUBLISHER / [Second, in red:] P [covering most of page] / [In black:] / OTHER / LITTLE / TALES / KARLSRUHE [slash] BADEN [Black dot] 1953

2 blank leaves, 6 leaves, 130 pp., 1 leaf, 2 blank leaves. 23.5 x 15.5 cm. Red cloth with yellow lettering, white, red, and yellow dust-wrapper with black and red lettering.

Published in Summer 1953. 450 copies printed. *On verso of title-leaf:* "none of these pieces has appeared in print before." Jargon #6.

Contents: The Walking Faces—How the Problem of What to Hold Cream in was Eventually Solved—The Scholar: The Insect—How Water First Came to be Tracked onto Bedroom Floors—The Historian of Orchards—Behind the Curtain, the Curtained Behind—Right Niece, Wrong Uncle - or Versa Vice—The Dolt and the Pretty Damsels—What's Sauce for the Tomato—In Old China—The Tale of Rosie Bottom—The Oeillander with an Indolent, Grease-Smeared Mustache—An Adventure with Jubiloso Giochevole—The Wolf that Cried Ohboy Ohboy—Sure Cure for a Cold—The Three Visitors—Moondogg and the One-Armed Dentist's Sister—Gaunt Eve in the Mornin'—The Unclaimed Beaver—He Didn't Know the Son was Loaded—Tat for Two—Bottoms Up—Chicken Fried in Honey—How Ostriches Came to have Throats

Long Enough to get Golf Balls Stuck in the Middle Of—A Case of Unmistakable Identity—Not all Towels Come from Turkey—Even the Kraken must Have his Spiel—How Pepper Came to be Discovered—How Carrottop Got a New Fur Coat—The Only Pair of Two-Pronged Rhinos in the World to Take up Polevaulting Professionally—The Evolution of the Hippopotamus—The Business, as Usual—The Hotel Blues—The Old Dog on the Doorstep—Banjo, Banjo . . . Who Stole that Little Ole Green Banjo?—When in Troy—Roberta: or the True Story of What Became of Crusoe's Wife—How Anthills Came to Wear Big Purple Sashes—The Substituted Substitutes—How the Slingshot Came to be Invented—Moonshine and Hawgjowl—The Number that Comes after Feve—The Professional Son—Portraits on a Pale Staircase—A First Lesson in Applied Logic—The Very Best Salesmen are not Born—Taking Hot Coals to Missouri—Perpetual Emotion—The Naval Base which Some Old Daymares Built—A Pasturized Scene—The Lady-Faced Sows—How to Tell A Vision—A Word about the Weather—The Bargain—The Foggy-Woggie Bo—Visit to a Suburb in Heaven—Night Picnic on the Beach—Eureka Europa!—A Fable about Fables—The Cock of All the World

b. *First Edition, special (painted) issue*

Title page, pagination, size, and contents as (a)

50 copies available with covers individually hand-painted by the author at $12.50.

A22   THE FAMOUS BOATING PARTY   1954

a. *First Edition, regular issue*

THE / FAMOUS / BOATING PARTY / AND OTHER POEMS IN PROSE / BY KENNETH PATCHEN / A NEW DIREC-TIONS BOOK

64 pp. 21.5 x 15 cm. Brown cloth with black lettering. Brown and orange dustwrapper with black lettering.

Published June 1 at $3.50. 2000 copies printed at the Blue Ridge Mountain Press in Parsippany, New Jersey.

Contents: Soon It Will—In Order To—On My Side—Evidence? What Evidence . . ?—Deathsong For A Maiden—Worn On The—Delighted With Bluepink—He Is An—Not Many Kingdoms Left—There Is The Hand—Yesterday They Tried—Now If You—Her Talents . . . Of—Rising A Little—To Be Charmed—It Takes Few Kinds—Childhood Of The Hero: Childhood Of The Hero 1, Childhood Of The Hero 2, Childhood Of The Hero 3, Childhood Of The Hero 4, Childhood Of The Hero 5, Childhood Of The Hero 6, Childhood Of The Hero 7, Childhood Of The Hero 8, Childhood Of The Hero 9—Seven

Nourishments Were—The Great Sled-Makers—Moon "Continued"—Wanderers Of The Pale Wood: Wanderers Of The Pale Wood 1, Wanderers Of The Pale Wood 2, Wanderers Of The Pale Wood 3, Wanderers Of The Pale Wood 4, Wanderers Of The Pale Wood 5, Wanderers Of The Pale Wood 6, Wanderers Of The Pale Wood 7, Wanderers Of The Pale Wood 8, Wanderers Of The Pale Wood 9, Wanderers Of The Pale Wood 10, Wanderers Of The Pale Wood 11, Wanderers Of The Pale Wood 12—In A Crumbling—Vines With Their—That Night The—Opening The Window—It Was Being—There "Are" Two—The Great Sadnesses—The Famous Boating Party—I Will Be—Sturdy Legs That— You Could Find—O What A Revolution!—Court Of First Appeal—Often Was It

b. *First Edition, special (painted) issue*

Title-page, pagination, size, contents as (a).

50 copies available with covers individually painted by the author at $10.00.

A23   POEMS OF HUMOR AND PROTEST   1954

a. *First Edition, first issue*

POEMS / OF / HUMOR / & / PROTEST / by / KENNETH PATCHEN / THE POCKET POETS SERIES: NUMBER THREE / City Lights Books / San Francisco

48 pp., 15.5 x 12.5 cm. Blue and white stiff paper wrappers with paper label and blue and white lettering.

Date of publication and number of copies unknown. 75¢. *On verso of dedication-leaf:* "NOTE The poems herein have been selected by the author from the following books, and the provenance of each poem is indicated in the table of contents by number: 1. *First Will And Testament*, 2. *Orchards, Thrones & Caravans*, 3. *Red Wine And Yellow Hair*, 4. *The Famous Boating Party*, 5. *Cloth Of The Tempest*, 6. *The Teeth Of The Lion*, 7. *The Dark Kingdom*." Later issues identified as such on verso of title-leaf and back cover.

Contents: The State Of The Nation (1)—Lonesome Boy Blues (2)—Portrait Of The Artist As An Interior Decorator (3)—Opening The Window (4)— Carnival Late At Night (5)—Eve Of St. Agony Or The Middleclass Was Sitting On Its Fat (1)—The Slums (5)—Fragment From 'A Little Play' (1)—The Grand Palace Of Versailles (6)—Pastoral (7)—Lunch Wagon On Highway 57 (5)— Elegy For The Silent Voices And The Joiners Of Everything (1)—There Are Two (4)—Wouldn't You Be After A Jaunt Of 964,000,000,000,000 Million Miles? (3)—I Don't Want To Startle You but they are going to kill most of us (1) —The Murder Of Two Men By A Young Kid Wearing Lemon-Colored Gloves (5)—The Hunted City V (1)—The Hunted City VII (1)—At The Gates Of The Lucky Town (5)—Street Corner College (1)—The Body Beside The Ties (1) —Investigation Of Certain Interesting Questions (5)—Hell Gate Bridge (6)— A Trueblue Gentleman (2)—Little Cannibal's Bedtimesong (2)—Man Is To

Man A Beast (1)—In Order To (4)—I Got The Fat Poet Into A Corner (1)—
The Man With The Golden Adam's Apple (5)—The Irate Songster (2)—The
Origin Of Baseball (6)—The Figure Motioned With Its Mangled Hand Towards
The Wall Behind It, and uttered a melancholy cry (1)

A24   GLORY NEVER GUESSES   1955

First Edition

[On black, in white print:] GLORY NEVER GUESSES / to Miriam
/ Being a collection of 18 poems / with decorations and drawings /
reproduced through silk screening / from the original MS. pages of
/ Kenneth Patchen / The Animal That Walks Sitting Down · Who
Are / You · In The Patient Eye · From "The Tea- / Kettle Sugges-
tion" · Keep It · Counsel For / The Offense . The Monument-Maker
· An Old / Lady Named Amber Sam · The Sun-Man / King Of
Logoona · Glory Never Guesses · If You / Can Lose Your Head ·
The Smallest Giant / In The World · To "Run The Crown" / House
On Horseback · The Moment / The Peacock · Garrity The Gam-
bling Man / SILK SCREEN REPRODUCTION BY FRANK
BACHER / IN A HAND-RUN EDITION OF 200 COPIES / ON
HANDMADE JAPANESE PAPERS / 10.⁰⁰ [Palo Alto, Cali-
fornia: Kenneth Patchen]

Unbound portfolio of 18 poems. Folder 38.5 x 45.5 cm., leaves 36 x 29 cm.
Some portfolios have an additional, variable sheet. Portfolio black with white
and gold design and lettering.

Published in November. 200 copies were produced on handmade Japanese
papers in a hand-run edition by Frank Bacher for Kenneth Patchen, and sold
by Patchen for $10.00. There was an over-run on some sheets, making individual
sheets available, and a number of these have found their way to the marketplace.

Contents: The Animal That Walks Sitting Down—Who Are You—Since In
The Patient Eye—From "The Tea-Kettle Suggestion—Keep It—Counsel for
the Offense—The Monument Maker—An Old Lady Named Amber Sam—
The Sun-Man—King of Logoona—Glory Never Guesses—If You Can Lose
Your Head—The World's Smallest Giant—To "Run the Crown"—House
on Horseback—The Moment—The Peacock—Garrity the Gambling Man

Note: Between the two silk screen portfolios, A24 and A25, 7200 pages were
printed. 5000 of these pages were then individually hand-colored by Patchen
in Japanese earth-colors. An average of thirteen of the eighteen pages in each
portfolio received this treatment, creating pages unique to each portfolio.
Pages which were hand-colored bear a stamp on the regular limitation sticker
on the back of the sheet reading "This paper hand-colored by Kenneth Patchen."
A few specimen pages also have survived, and bear a stamp in large letters to
that effect.

A25   A SURPRISE FOR THE   1956
                          BAGPIPE PLAYER
First Edition

[On red, in white print:] A Surprise For The Bagpipe Player / to
Miram / [In gold:] Being a collection of 18 poems / with decora-
tions and drawings / reproduced through silk screening / from the
original MS. pages of / Kenneth Patchen / [In white:] Unless There
Are Flowers · O Honor The Bird / "Listen" Is A Purple Elephant
· What Indeed / The Little Bug Angel · The Clock-Bear · With /
One Tiny Stick — The Question Is — Quick / Thinker — Tiger Con-
templating A Cake · The / Man With The Gardenias · Behind
Every / Really Throughtful Chicken — The Giraffe Of Sofas /
Sleeper Under The Tree — Binding The Quiet / The Broom Of Bells
A Surprise For The / Bagpipe Player — The Great Fly Fleet / [In
gold:] SILK SCREEN REPRODUCTION BY FRANK BACHER
/ IN A HAND-RUN EDITION OF 200 COPIES / ON HAND-
MADE JAPANESE PAPERS / 10⁰⁰ [Palo Alto, California: Ken-
neth Patchen]

> Unbound portfolio of 18 poems. Folder 38.5 x 45.5 cm., leaves 36 x 29 cm. Some
> portfolios have an additional, variable sheet. Portfolio red with gold and white
> design and lettering.
>
> Printed at the same time as A24, but not published until early 1956. 200 copies
> were produced on handmade Japanese papers in a hand-run edition by Frank
> Bacher for Kenneth Patchen, and sold by Patchen for $10.00. There was an over-
> run on some sheets, making individual sheets available, and a number of these
> have found their way to the marketplace.
>
> *Contents:* Unless There Are Flowers—O Honor the Bird—"Listen" is a Purple
> Elephant—What Indeed—The Little Bug Angel—The Clock-Bear—With One
> Tiny Stick—The Question Is—Quick Thinker—Tiger Contemplating a Cake—
> The Man With the Gardenias— In Back of Every Really Thoughtful Chicken—
> The Giraffe of Sofas—Sleeper Under the Tree—Binding the Quiet—The Broom
> of Bells—A Surprise for the Bagpipe Player—The Great Fly Fleet
>
> *Note:* See note for A24

A26   HURRAH FOR ANYTHING   1957

A. *First Edition, regular issue*

[Title spread over three pages. First:] HURRAH / JARGON 21 /
[Second:] FOR / POEMS & DRAWINGS BY / KENNETH

PATCHEN / [Third:] ANYTHING / PUBLISHED BY / JONATHAN WILLIAMS / HIGHLANDS 1957

1 blank leaf, 4 leaves, 13-62 pp., 1 blank leaf. 21 x 14 cm. Grey self-wraps with blue lettering.

Published at $1.75. 2500 copies printed.

Contents: Where?—Never Like This Back in Marblehead—Bringing Home The Little Bride— The Peaceful Lier—Don't Tell Me—We Meet—I Am Timothy The Lion—Travelers Of Necessity—Far Out—What's This I Hear About Charlie?—O! O!—I Am The Chicken—It Is The Hour—When Is A Stalker Not A Stalker?—Perhaps It Is Time—The "Greater Good"—Where Tribute Is Due —Players In Low See—Only Cherries?—FLAPjaCKS ON THE PIAzzA—All The Roary Night—One Who Hopes—How Come?—Who Can Tell?—A Riddle For The 1st Of The Month—A Morning In Bic-Bic . . . In The Good Old Days— News From Back Of Yonder—Dogs Boating—I Went To The City—A WordTo The Sufficient— Yes, Bluebell, This Time It Is Goodbye—The Cowboy Who Went To College—The Little Man With Wooden Hair—The Man-At-A-Table —The Tame Streetcar Conductor—The Wily Cartographer—The Careless Little Spy—The Forgetful Little Commuter—The Litle Man Who Saw A Grass —The Loyal Stanley Steamerite—The Old Bronchobuster—The Man Who Was Shorter Than Himself—The Celery-Flute Player—The Goggle-Eyed Rabbit-Counter—Prominent Couple Believed Permanently Stuck To Porch— On The Parkbench (sleeps a small bird-shaped man)—On The Parkbench (sleeps a tiger)—And With The Sorrows Of This Joyousness—An "Impression Gazoom"—Like I Told You

b. *First Edition, special (painted) issue*

Title page, pagination, size, and contents as (a)

100 copies "prepared and painted by Kenneth Patchen" and sold for $6.00.

A27   WHEN WE WERE HERE TOGETHER   1957

A. *First Edition, regular issue*

WHEN WE / WERE HERE / TOGETHER / KENNETH / PATCHEN / [Device] A NEW DIRECTIONS BOOK

112 pp., 25.5 x 15.5 cm. Blue cloth with black lettering. Buff, green and blue dust-wrapper with black lettering.

Published on November 10 at $3.50. 2000 copies printed at the Walpole Printing Office. *On verso of title-leaf:* "Certain of these poems were first printed in *The Bridge, Liberation, Ark-II, The Miscellaneous Man, The Needle, Zero,* and

Poetry; later printings include a number of anthology and translation appearances. Forty-two poems comprised the volume, *Orchards, Thrones & Caravans,* which was issued by The Print Workshop, Woodstock, N.Y., in a small edition restricted to private distribution: That is, copies were not offered for store sales, and of course no review copies were sent out."

Contents: Wide, Wide in the Rose's Side—Beautiful You Are—Give You a Lantern—First Came The Lion-Rider—Under A Tree—The Everlasting Contenders—All Is Safe . . . —A Matchstick-Viewed-Without-Regard-to-its-Outer-Surface—The Great Birds—"And I, Too, Am Only a Little Clerk," He Said—The Unanswering Correspondences—Lowellville Cemetery: Twilight—Day of Rabblement—A Becoming for the Curly Blue Bear—Backcountry Blues—And Her Look Touching The Air—The Cruelkind Swans—At Grandmother's Wake —Two Ghosts Together—Always Another Viewpoint—Lonesome Boy Blues— A Message from the Assistant Chief of the Fly Nation—Song of th' Little Shuckin' Boy—Catfish River Lullaby—O Kind Watchers Come—In the Courtyard of Secret Life—The Green Fires—The Oldest Conversation—The Bird-Queen—A Vanishing Institution—Little Cannibal's Bedtimesong—What Splendid Birthdays—It's a Smallworld—All the Flowery—O What Do You See— We Bathed Him—Flowers to the house—Morning, My Prince, the Eye that Walks—Folly of Clowns—A Jungle Village—The Irate Songster—Lament and Lullaby—Should Be Sufficient—My Pretty Animals—Who Walks There?— The Magical Mouse—A Trueblue Gentleman—O She Is as Lovely-Often— Behond the Dark Cedars—Down in Ol' Dontcaradama—Who'll That Be— So Near—An Unexpected Impasse—In the Moonlight—An Easy Decision— Encounter at Nightfall—O the Sledbird Rides—Watching Neighbors' Children —For Miriam—Limpidity of Silences—The Unreturning Hosts—The Constant Bridegrooms—Where Every Prospect—But of Life?—The Wonderful Sun!—So Be It—What There Is—Flowers Riding—O Now the Drenched Land Wakes—The Only Thing that Was Full that Night Was the Moon—The Sequel —Just Outside Tombstone—"Gentle and Giving" and Other Sayings—The Most Hen—Autobiographical Note—The Dog-Board—Another Hamlet Is Heard From—It's All Graft Anyway—Let Me In—It's Because Your Heart Is Pure, Honey—When We Were Here Together

b. *First Edition, special (painted) issue*

Title page, pagination, and contents as (a). Boards extended to 25.5 cm.

75 copies were available with covers individually hand-painted by the author and sold for $15.00.

A28   POEMSCAPES   [1957] 1958

a. *Pirated Edition*

KENNETH PATCHEN / POESAGGI / VERSIONE DO LINA ANGIOLETTI / IMMAGINI DI ENRICO BAJ / MILANO [Italy] / EDIZIONI DEL TRIAGOLO / 1957

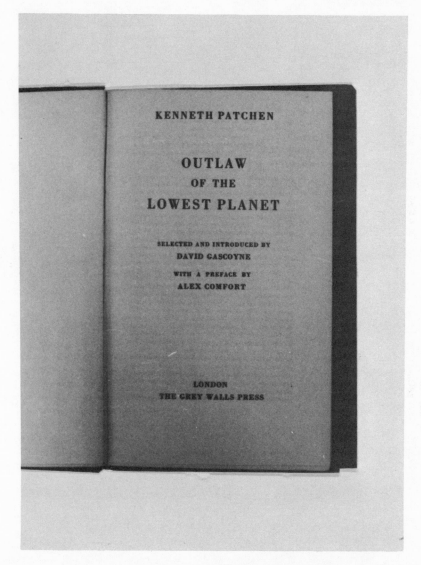

Title Page of *Outlaw of the Lowest Planet* (1946). A9.

Title Page of *Sleepers Awake* (1946). Allc.

1 blank leaf, 2 leaves, 7-26 pp., 1 leaf. Red paper wrappers.

Publication data unavailable. It did in fact appear before any other edition. However, it was unauthorized and included only those poems which had previously appeared in print. The poems are in Italian.

Contents: Poemscapes: xvii—xviii—xxiii—xxv—xxvii—xxviii—xxxvii— x1—x1ii

b. *First Edition, special ("Gold and Gray") issue*

[Title-page consists of two facing pages. First Page:] POEM- / KENNETH / JONATHAN WILLIAMS PUBLISHER 19 / [Second page:] SCAPES / PATCHEN / 58 HIGHLANDS, NORTH CAROLINA

4 leaves, [42] pp., 1 leaf. Signed by Patchen, and including a hand-written poem.

Published in January. 42 copies of this issue available. *Colophon:* "First printing. by the Stephens Press, Asheville, NC. January 1958." Jargon #11.

Contents: Poemscapes: I through XLII

c. *First Edition, special (painted) issue.*

Title page, pagination, size, and contents as (b).

Boards with original paintings by Patchen. 75 copies, sold at $7.00.

d. *First Edition, regular issue*

Title page, pagination, size, and contents as (b).

Printed stiff white self-wrappers with orange and blue lettering. Published at $1.75. 325 copies printed.

A29   BECAUSE IT IS   1960

First Edition

BECAUSE IT IS / POEMS AND DRAWINGS BY / KENNETH PATCHEN / [Drawing] / A NEW DIRECTIONS PAPERBOOK

5 leaves, [1] — 83 pp., 1 leaf. 20 x 13.75 cm. White pictorial wrappers with black and white lettering.

Published April 21 at $1.25. 5000 copies printed at the Murray Printing Company, Forge Village, Mass. *On verso of title-leaf:* "New Directions Paperbook Original, first published as ND Paperbook No. 83, 1960 . . . These poems and drawings have not been published before." To date, seven additional printings of 5000; later printings identified as such on verso of title-leaf and upper right corner of back cover. Cover by Ray Johnson with a drawing by the author.

Contents: BECAUSE to understand one must begin somewhere—BECAUSE they were very poor that winter—BECAUSE she felt bashful with palm trees—BECAUSE everybody looked so friendly I ran—BECAUSE the zebra-plant bore spotted cubs—BECAUSE all the forests were playing leapfrog—BECAUSE I didn't mean no harm, Mister—BECAUSE the street sat there scratching himself—BECAUSE we make out when we're in—BECAUSE the flyby-night peered into the washtub—BECAUSE sometimes you can't always be so—BECAUSE a door in the hill opened—BECAUSE a firtree shook hands with Orion—BECAUSE going nowhere takes a long time—BECAUSE the ground-creature looked so sad—BECAUSE the boy-headed lark played one—BECAUSE my hands hear the flowers thinking—BECAUSE sunset came at half-past noon—BECAUSE his sister saw Shakespeare in the moon—BECAUSE he kept imagining a pensive rabbit—BECAUSE his other dog was a horse—BECAUSE he was thinking of a bumblebee—BECAUSE his friend claimed there weren't any—BECAUSE it's good to keep things straight—BECAUSE growing a mustache was pretty tiring—BECAUSE above the clouds little frogooses floated—BECAUSE their bells never tolled the truth—BECAUSE where they planted skygreen leopards grew—BECAUSE the nervous vine wouldn't twine—BECAUSE sometimes the handwriting eats away the wall—BECAUSE the small man was a Stranger—BECAUSE Mr. Flowers the boatman sailed walls—BECAUSE the whole world was on fire—BECAUSE today's monkey may well be tomorrow's tueslock—BECAUSE there are roses, swans, and herbugazelles—BECAUSE in this sorrowing statue of flesh—BECAUSE it didn't like the story anyway—BECAUSE to really ponder one needs wonder—BECAUSE a cow chewed off the trainwheels—BECAUSE everybody's clock keeps a different time—BECAUSE he liked to be at home

A 30   THE MOMENT   1960

First Edition

[No title-leaf]

THE MOMENT [Palo Alto, California: Kenneth Patchen]

Bound edition of portfolios A24 and A25. 38.5 x 32.5 cm. Signed by Patchen. White half-leather and tan buckram with black label printed in white, purple, and tan.

Published [signed] December 5. 42 copies hand-bound at the printshop of Henry Geiger, Alhambra, California.

Contents: Glory Never Guesses, and *A Surprise for the Bagpipe Player*

Note: See note for A24

A31   THE LOVE POEMS   1960

First Edition

The / LOVE POEMS / of / KENNETH / PATCHEN / [Device] / The Pocket Poets Series: Number 13 / CITY LIGHTS BOOKS / San Francisco

48 pp. 17 x 13 cm. Blue and white stiff paper wrappers with blue and white lettering.

No publication data. $1.00. *On verso of title-leaf:* "This selection was made from the following volumes, and the provenance of each poem is recorded in the table of contents by number: 1. *Orchards, Thrones & Caravans,* 2. *First Will & Testament,* 3. *Cloth Of The Tempest,* 4. *The Dark Kingdom,* 5. *When We Were Here Together,* 6. *Pictures Of Life And Of Death,* 7. *The Teeth Of The Lion,* 8. *Red Wine & Yellow Hair,* 9. *The Famous Boating Party.* Books numbered two, five, seven, eight, and nine were originally published by New Directions—in 1939, 1957, 1942, 1949, and 1954, respectively. Number three was published by Harper & Brothers in 1943; number four by Harriss & Givens in 1942; number six by Padell Publishers in 1946 and finally number one appeared in a privately subscribed edition by The Print Workshop in 1952. New printings of numbers two, three, and four were issued by Padell Publishers in 1946. Numbers one and seven are at present out of print." Later issues identified as such on verso of title-leaf and bottom of back cover.

Contents: For Miriam (as beautiful as the hands)—'As Frothing Wounds Of Roses' (2)—'O My Darling Troubles Heaven With Her Loveliness' (3)—Fall Of The Evening Star (2)—'She Is The Prettiest Of Creatures' (3)—'Be Music, Night' (3)—'We Go Out Together Into The Staring Town' (2)—'The Snow Is Deep On The Ground' (3)—23rd Street Runs Into Heaven (2)—She Had Concealed Him (2)—Five Early Poems: (2), 'This Room Has Mystery Like Trance', "Your Name Includes The Shadow Flight of Birds", 'I Know The Hair, Tissue, Skin', 'It Is A Lonely Walk Into The Mind's Retreat', Geography Of Music—And What With The Blunders (2)—'Beautiful You Are' (1)—'For Losing Her Love' (4)—As She Was Thus Alone (2)—'O She Is As Lovely-Often' (5)—'While The Sun Still Spends Its Money' (6)—'O My Love The Pretty Towns' (7)—'From My High Love I Look At That Poor World There (4)—'O When I Take My Love Out Walking' (8)—Creation (2)—'O Now The Drenched Land Wakes' (5)—Religion Is That I Love You (2)—'When All That Changes Is The World' (New)—Heart (3)—'Little Birds Sit On Your Shoulders' (5)—'Where My Stag-Antlered Love' (4)—To Say If You Love Someone—'O Sleeping Lay The Maiden Snow' (6)—In Judgement Of The Leaf (2)—The Character Of Love Seen As A Search For The Lost (2)—'Do I Not Deal With Angels' (7)—'As We Are So Wonderfully Done With Each Other' (4)—'The Sea Is Awash With Roses' (4)—The Great Birds (5)—There Are Not Many Kingdoms Left (9)

A 32   DOUBLEHEADER   1966

a. *First Edition, first issue*

[Two books back to back, thus a title page on each end of book. First
title page extends over two pages. First page:] POEMSCAPES /
Kenneth Patchen / [Second page:] [Vertical:] AND [Horizontal:] A
LETTER TO GOD / New Directions / [Second title page, on other
side of book, extending over three pages. First page:] HURRAH /
[Second page:] FOR / Poems & Drawings by / KENNETH
PATCHEN / [Third page:] ANYTHING / New Directions

> 5 leaves, [21] pp., 1 leaf, 45-55 pp.; 62 pp. Black and white printed wrappers.

> Published at $1.35. 4500 printed. *On verso of each title-leaf:* "Copyright 1958,
> 1957, 1946 by Kenneth Patchen." *Hallelujah Anyway* not mentioned in descrip-
> tive notes on page following *Poemscapes* title-leaf.

> *Contents:* Poemscapes [A29]—A Letter to God [C3]—Hurrah for Anything
> [A27]

b. *First Edition, later issues*

> As (a), but expanded copyright notice, *Hallelujah Anyway* included in descrip-
> tive notes.

A 33   HALLELUJAH ANYWAY   1966

a. *First Edition*

Drawing / HALLELUJAH ANYWAY / KENNETH PATCHEN
/ A NEW DIRECTIONS BOOK

> 1 blank leaf, 3 leaves, [88] pp., 2 blank leaves. 21 x 14 cm. Maroon paper boards
> with glossy finish, picture-poem on cover; black, white, blue, and red lettering.
> Dust-wrapper same as binding.

> Published on March 27 at $7.50. 2000 copies printed.

> *Contents:* When This Is It—They Are So Happy—The concerns of the heart—
> The Word Is Nothing That Can't Be Known—Come—All at once is what eter-
> nity is—Pleasantly We shall remain—Ask the Grass—So when that nosey con-
> ductor comes round—Man Is Not a Town—Elephants and Eskimos—The
> World's Not Enough Really—the day has followed me about—My Program?—
> & so the little fieldmouse said—Inside the Flower—The Ground Keeper's Dog
> and the Castle-Master's Cat—Love (Which Includes Poetry)—What the story

tells itself—Ah! here comes the 9th one—Tribute to a Grandfadder Foof—
Imagine Seeing You Here—Of Course They Will Win—You Can't Leave Leave
the Doughnut Whole—Little Chief Son-Of-A-Gun-Don't-Give-A-Shoot—
Now is Then's Only Tomorrow—Oh Come Now—I have a funny feeling—The
birds are very careful of this world—The Burso "Dockle"—Been driven from our
radioactive temples—Shaggy Balls of Fur, Enos!—It Wasn't So Bad Really—
And The Some Fellows—That Petey D Croos is a shy one—I Got Me The Blue
Dawg Blues—That's Nice—Now, When I Get Back Here—The One Who
Comes to Question Himself—Tree-Sleeping Behind-Lectures—The Day
Dreams Of A King—In The Long Run—ead, pow!—I Proclaim—O Take heart,
My Brothers—Sure Is One Peculiar Way To Run A Ballgame—What can you
do up here—Peace or Perish—And To Think It All Started Out Like Any Other
World—In Perkko's Grotto—The Walker Standing—In the hippodrome—
the Continuous Christ—The Lion Part—The red flesh of the Rose—Billy Besto
& Mr Bug—You Know, Somehow I Think, Old Pal—The Best Hope—The
Walking-Away World—I Am The Ghost—An interview with the Floating Man
—Hallelujah is my name—Who've you been today—Had General Grant Been
A Xmas Tree—Check! Questions Are The Best Things I Answer, Bub—All
Right, You May Alight—The Scene Of The Crime—Pretty Soon Comes The
Punch Line—There Isn't Much More To Tell—No Denial Of Rumor—You've
faced wrong, that's what's the matter—Upon the book of the Waters—Unless
you clock in—Is that all that's wrong!—A Dream of Goethe Dancing—Only A
Bit Longer—Snow is the only one of us that leaves no tracks—A Something-
Like-That Look—Whaleagle Rider—The Easy Hat-Eye—Man Would You
Just Look At Your Leaders—all is as it is not—The Soup—Rode Him Out of a
Dream—Whever You're Ready—Well, if you don't want me to buy Philly for
you—he's either going away—A feeling of passionate mercy

Note: Patchen had planned a "Painted Book" edition of *Hallelujah Anyway,*
but was foiled by the binding. Nothing would stick to it. He tried steaming off
the coating, cutting it off, melting it, and covering it with paper. A few remain-
ing copies show the efforts: grey paper of the sort he liked to use clinging to the
endpapers.

b. *First Paperback Edition* (1966)

As (a), but printed wrappers.

5500 printed; to date four additional printings of 5500. Later printings identified
on verso of title-leaf.

A34   THE COLLECTED POEMS   1968

A. *First Edition*

THE / COLLECTED / POEMS / OF / KENNETH / PATCHEN
/ A NEW DIRECTIONS BOOK

1 blank leaf, 4 leaves, 503 [1] pp., 1 blank leaf. 21 x 14.5 cm. Red cloth with gold
lettering. White dust-wrapper with red and black lettering.

2000 copies printed at $12.50. *On verso of title-leaf:* "First Edition. Design of Book and Jacket from suggestions of the poet." Second printing of 2000 copies identified as such on title-leaf verso.

Contents: Before the Brave (1936), "Let Us Have Madness Openly"—Among Ourselves and with All Nations—That We Here Highly Resolve—When in the Course of Human Events—It Is for Us the Living—The Last Full Measure of Devotion—Thus Far So Nobly Advanced—We Mutually Pledge to Each Other —We Hold These Truths to Be Self-evident—Prayer Not to Go to Paradise with the Asses—The World Will Little Note—1935—A Letter to a Policeman in Kansas City—The Magic Car—We Leave You Pleasure—Letter to the Old Men—Demonstration—History Is a Throne and a Gate—All the Day—A Letter to Those Who Are about to Die—The Ladder—Night Has Been as Beautiful as Virginia—The Firing—This Man Was Your Brother—A Letter on the Use of Machine Guns at Weddings—The Other Side: The Green Home—The Mechanical Heart—Nocturne for the Heirs of Light—Having Been Near—There's a Train Leaving Soon—Loyalty Is the Life you Are—Note For A Diary—Country Excursion—My Generation Reading the Newspapers—A Letter to the Inventors of a Tradition—Dostoyevsky—A Letter to the Liberals—A Letter to the Young Men—Leaflet (One)—Leaflet (Two)—Poem in the Form of a Letter: to Lauro de Bosis—This Early Day—Ark: Angelus: Anvil—We Must Be Slow —Fields of Earth—A Letter on Liberty—Class of 1934—The Stranger—Farewell to the Bluewoman—Pick Up the Evening Paper—Joe Hill Listens to the Praying—A World Whose Sun Retreats before the Brave—*First Will & Testament* (1939), "As Frothing Wounds of Roses" for Miriam—Poem—A Small But Brilliant Fire Blazed In The Grate—Avarice And Ambition Only Were The First Builders Of Towns And Founders Of Empire—He Thought of Mad Ellen's Ravings and of the Wretched Skeleton on the Rock—Fall of the Evening Star— Behold, One Of Several Little Christs—The Queer Client And The Forest-Inn— She Had Concealed Him In A Deep Dark Cave—The Fox—You May All Go Home Now—Creation—The Hangman's Great hands—The Poor Child with the Hooked Hands—But The Images Of His Former Dreams Still Haunted Him—As She Was Thus Alone In The Clear Moonlight—And What With The Blunders—To Whom It May Concern—Though I Had Much More To Say— Boxers Hit Harder When Women Are Around—Crossing on Staten Island Ferry—The Character of Love Seen as a Search for the Lost—Street Corner College—Poem Written after Reading Certain Poets Sired by the English School and Bitched by the C.P.—The State of the Nation—The Soldier and the Star—All the Bright Foam of Talk—I Can't Understand! I Can't Understand!— The Deer and the Snake—Fifth Dimension—In Memory of Kathleen—I Never had Any Other Desire So Strong—Religion Is That I Love You—Niobe— Palms for a Catholic Child—Inasmuch as War Is Not for Women—The Old Lean Over The Tombstones—Heine, Too, Lived in Germany—Do the Dead Know What Time It Is?—Nice Day for a Lynching—Man Is To Man A Beast— Elegy for the Silent Voices and the Joiners of Everything—He Is Guarded By Crowds And Shackled With Formalities—Death Will Amuse Them—I Got The Fat Poet Into A Corner—The Quantity of Mercy—Eve of St. Agony, or the Middle Class Was Sitting on Its Fat—Fog—If We Are to Know Where We Live —Autumn Is the Crows' Time—And He Had Wilder Moments—The Overworld—Plow Horses—Career for a Child of Five—Hymn to a Trench Gun— 23rd Street Runs into Heaven—Eight Early Poems; I, II, III The Sea Has Caves

And Urns, IV, V, VI Fragment From "A Schoolboy's Odyssey"; VII Geography Of Music, VIII At The New year— And In Another Place Uses The Same Phrase—He Was Alone (As In Reality) Upon His Humble Bed—All That Night Lights Were Seen Moving In Every Direction—Tomorrow—The Executions in Moscow—The Body Beside the Ties—Portrait on an American Theme—Peter's Diary in Goodentown, Peter Records the Sparrow's Falling Feather, The Day-Mists Are Strewn With Us, Spring In Goodentown, Porest Near Goodentown, Peter Reads Emerson:, Bya Deena, Peter Gains A Son, Peter Reports On Himself, Peter's Little Daughter Dies, The Shelling of Goodentown—The Figure Motioned With Its Mangled hand Toward The Wall Behind It—Can the Harp Shoot Through Its Propellers?—On The South-West Coast Of Erehwemos Stands A Romantic Little Village—Meditation of My Lady of Sorrows—Stayed No Longer in the Place Than to Hire a Guide for the Next Stage—In Judgment of the Leaf—Biography of Sourthern Rain—The Black Panther and the Little Boy—I Suddenly Became Conscious That This Thing Was Looking at Me Intently—"These Have Gone with Silent Hands, Seeking" —I Don't Want To Startle You—Harrowed By These Apprehensions He Resolved To Commit Himself To The Mercy Of The Storm—Early In The Morning—The Hunted City, I, II, III, IV, V, VI, VII—*The Teeth of the Lion* (1942), For Miriam (Do I not deal with angels)—Kibali-Ituri—The Grand Palace of Versailles—The Reason for Skylarks—Turner—"The Lions of Fire Shall Have Their Hunting"—Midnight Special—"I Have Lighted the Candles, Mary"—The Origin of Baseball—A Theory of Nato-geography as Advanced by the Tiaphidian Man, With a Comment on the Character of His Penal System—Cleveland, Oh?—"O My Love the Pretty Towns"—Moon, Sun, Sleep, Birds, Live—Poly—An Almost-True Story—"Under the Green Ledge"—Legend for a Little Child— *The Dark Kingdom* (1942), For Miriam (The sea is awash with roses)—A Temple—The Forms of Knowledge—The Rites of Darkness—The Watcher—These Unreturning Destinies—The Second People—"Into Another Mission"—The Cloth of the Tempest—"In the Footsteps of the Walking Air"—The Village Tudda—Irkalla's White Caves—"Where My Stag-Antlered Love Moves"—The Lasting Seasons—The Expectant Shelters—Meben—A Devotion—The Crowded Net—The Naked land—"As We Are So Wonderfully Done with Each Other"—The Manifold Fusions—The Blind Maidens of Our Home lessness—Heaven and Earth—"There Is Nothing False in Thee"—Continuation of the Landscape—"From My High Love I Look at That Poor World There"—"For Losing her Love All Would I Profane"—"We Go Out Together into the Staring Town"—We Are Not Worthy, Lord—Virtue—The Meaning of Life—Paxdominisit Sem Pervobiscum Etcumspiri Tuto—"The Wolf of Winter"—Like a Mourningless Child—The Known Soldier—How God Was Made—An Examination into Life and Death—Lenada—What Happened in the Camps—"I Suggest That This Day Be Made Holy"—Saturday Night in the Parthenon—The Intimate Guest—The Spirit of Noplace—The Outlaw of the Lowest Planet—Pastoral—O Howling Cells—O Everlasting Queen!—Written after Reading an Item in the Paper about a Young Lady Who Went Made upon Foresaking Her Lover. He Is Here Assumed to Speak—Preparation for the Highest Being—The Climate of War—What the Grecian Earns—"Sovereign of the Wilderness"—Waking into Sleep—The Permanent Migrations—Fellow Soul, Sound Hunting To Thy Immeasurable Heart—Those upon Whom God Has Labored—There Is One Who Watches—In Your Body All Bodies Lie—*Cloth of the Tempest* (1943), Cruelties of the Sportive Power—November in

Ohio—Ectasy of the Pure—"As in the Green Sky"—Progress to a View of Life—The Destruction of Carthage—The Pathway—To the Jewish People—Trial Of The Chill Giant—"In Shadings of an Obscure Punishment"—The Age of Pericles—Mirru—The Empire of Persia—Lao Tsze—The Education of the Waters—Egypt—The Unfufilling Brightnesses—The Shapes and Intensities of This Man, This Confucius—The Appian Way—Attila—The First Crusades —"The Snow Is Deep on the Ground"—Gautama in the Deer Park at Benares —Mohammed—To Be Holy, be Wholly Your Own—The Authority of Krajova —The Slums—It Was A Bomby Evening—The Abandoned Forest—Pleasures of This Gentle Day—"The Mule of Water"—The Unnatural History of Peru—The Nervousness of Memory—Lunch Wagon on Highway 57—The Battle of Unameit—The Man with the Golden Adam's Apple—Thinking Rock—"She Is the Prettiest of Creatures"—Where Two O'clock Came From—"When the Stones Burst into Flame"—"There Are No Losses"—May I Ask You a Question, Mr. Youngstown Sheet & Tube?—How Old The World Is!—"O My Darling Troubles Heaven with her Loveliness"—"Of the Same Beauty Were Stars Made"—I Sent A Mental to My Love—She Knows It's Raining—"For Whose Adornment"—"Be Music, Night"—The Impatient Explorer—"In Horror the God-thrown Lie"—Have You Killed Your Man for Today?—"Hold Thy Tongue, Death!"—Investigation of Certain Interesting Questions—Anna Karenina and the Love-sick River—The Murder of Two men by a Young Kid Wearing Lemon-colored Gloves—The Knowledge of Old Towns—"The Darts of the Wee Blind Lass"—"And When Freedom Is Achieved . . ."—"O Terrible Is The Highest Thing"—To Say if You Love Someone—Now I Went Down to the Ringside and Little Henry Armstrong Was There—My Coat Is Dirty—"Ah, God, Dear Brother, the Mild and FrowningRose"—"House, and a Dead Man in It"—How To be An Army—The Tribes of Rakala—Easy Rider—Something Watches You—The Colony of the Sun—"The Animal I Wanted"—O Fill Your Sack With Tiger Cubs—What Is the Beautiful?—For the Mother of My Mother's Mother—"These Are My Great Ones"—Lives of the Swan—Instructions for Angels—The Billion Freedoms—"How Silent Are the Things of Heaven"—The Continual Ministry of Thy Anger—"It Is Big Inside a Man"—"Rest, Heart of the Tired World"—"O Fiery River'—*An Astonished Eye Looks Out of the Air* (1945), "The Stars Go to Sleep So Peacefully"—"I Always Return to This Place"—The Dazzling Burden—This Summer Day—It Depends on Whose Science—"Beings so Hideous That the Air Weeps Blood"—I Feel Drunk All the Time—"Poems Which Are Written by the Soul"—Blood of the Sun—At the Entrance to the Other World—"The Way Men Live Is a Lie"—*Pictures of Life and Death* (1946), For Miriam (O my dearest While the sun still spends its fabulous money)—O All down within the Pretty Meadow—The Lovers—Toss at Their Wondrous Play—"I'd Want Her Eyes to Fill with Wonder"—Shadows and Spring Flowers—So It Ends—The Valley-sleeper, the Children, the Snakes, and the Giant—"Here Might Have Been the Thinking of Mountains"—You Must Have Some Idea Where They've Gone—"What I'd Like to Know Is"—The Strange, Moving Lights Of People Handle Holinesses Unknown—The Daft Little Shoe Clerk Decided It Would Be Fun to Go Up and See What Things Are Like above the Sky— "Pretty Glow on the Water"—Winter Poem—Yellow Stones - Sea of Majestic Dives—Don't Wash Your Hair in the Streetcar, Nora Dear—"O Sleeping Falls the Maiden Snow"—All the Roses of the World—Sure There Is Food—"Christ! Christ! That the World"—History in a Minor Kay—*Panels for the Walls of Heaven*

(1946), A Man Lives Here—Waiting Can Be Pretty Lousy—Not if He Has Any Sense, He Won't Be Back—"Peace in This Green Field"—I Have No Place to Take Thee—I Care What Happens—Each Is Alone, Each is Everything—A Time to Believe—The Builders—"No One Ever Works Alone"—*Red Wine & Yellow Hair* (1949), The Hunter—The New Being—A Lost Poem—And a Man Went Out Alone—"Blind'd Be the Last of Men"—Hovenweep, Frogs and Queens, The Krelullin—"White Lions Are Roaring on the Water"—Late-summer Blues—The Radiance in a Dark Wood—Portrait of the Artist as an Interior Decorator—"Breathe on the Living"—Weekend Bathers—The Question Is, Who Is Afraid of What?—"Put the Rest Away, O Put the Rest Away"—The Lute in the Attic—Fog over the Sea and the Sun Going Down—The Little Black Train—To the Tune of an Ancient Song—A Plate of Steaming Fish—The Orange Bears—Shapes—"This Summer Earth"—After an Old Song—"O When I Take My Love Out Walking"—Wouldn't You Be after a Jaunt of 964,000,000,000,000 Million Miles?—If a Poem Can Be Headed into Its Proper Current Someone Will Take It within His Heart to the Power and the Beauty of Everybody—Down in the Lone Valley—How Jimsey O'Roon and Peter Stack, Coal Miners, Came to Be Put in the Ferbettville (Pa.) Jail Early One Saturday Night—Lament for the Makers of Songs—Old Man—Two for History—Poor Gorrel—Family Portrait—An Old Pair of Shoes—The Event at Konna—Winter at the Inn—"Do Me That Love"—Red Wine and Yellow Hair—*Orchards, Thrones & Caravans* (1952), For Miriam (As Beautiful as the hands—But of Life?—The Green Fires—Lowellville Cemetary: Twilight—Watching Neighbors' Children—The Constant Bridergrooms—The Unreturning Hosts —Folly of Clowns—All the Flowery—At Grandmother's Wake—Two Ghosts Together—Where Every Prospect—It's My Town!—Who Walks There?—So Be It—Under a Tree—Beautiful You Are—It's a Smallworld—Should Be Sufficient—Day of Rabblement—The Magical Mouse—Lonesome Boy Blues—My Pretty Animals—Little Cannibal's Bedtimesong—All Is Safe . . .—The Oldest Conversation—A Trueblue Gentleman—Always Another Viewpoint—The Irate Songster—The Cruelkind Swans—A Vanishing Institution—Limpidity of Silences—What There Is—An Easy Decision—The Unanswering Correspondences—The Bird-Queen—The Everlasting Contenders—What Splendid Birthdays—Encounter at Nightfall—*The Famous Boating Party* 1954), Not Many Kingdoms Left—Childhood of the Hero—Soon It Will—In Order to—Evidence? What Evidence . . .?—Yesterday They Tried—On My Side—Deathsong for a Maiden——Worn on The—Delighted with Bluepink—He Is An—The Great-Sledmakers—"There Is the Hand"—Now if You—Opening the Window—Vines with Their—That Night The—Rising a Little—Her Talents . . . Of—O What a Revolution!—There Are Two—It Was Being—To Be Charmed—It Takes Few Kinds—Sturdy Legs, That—Often Was It—Wanderers of the Pale Wood—Moon "Continued"—The Great Sadnesses—Court of First Appeal—In a Crumbling—*When We Were Here Together* (1957), For Miriam (Little birds sit on your shoulders)—"First Came the Lion-Rider"—Backcountry Blues—A Matchstick-Viewed-without-Regard-to-Its-Outer-Surface—"Give You a Lantern—A Message from the Assistant Chief of the Fly People—The Great Birds—"And Her Look Touching the Air"—"And I, Too, Am Something of a Stranger Here, My Friend"—The Curly Blue Buppo—"O Kind Watchers Came"—So Near-and Yet . . .—"O She Is as Lovely-Often as Every Day"—Flowers to the House—Down in Ol' Dontcara-dama—Catfish River Lullaby—Beyond the Dark Cedars—"O the Sledbird

Rides over the Willow"—Ohio River Blues—In the Courtyard of Secret Life—
Just outside Tombstone—It's Because Your Heart Is Pure, Honey—Morning,
My Prince-the Eye That Walks—When We Were Here Together—"O Now
the Drenched Land Wakes"—The Rose of Life—"Who'll That Be"—Auto-
biographical Note—"Let Me In!"—"Gentle and Giving" and Other Sayings—
"Wide, Wide in the Rose's Side"

Notes: This volume covered Patchen's books only through 1957. Even among
these books, he selected, rather than collected. A second volume was planned,
primarily to collect the picture-poems, but was never published.

b. *First Paperback Edition* (1968)

Title-page as (a)

4 leaves, 504 pp. Printed stiff paper wrappers, Photograph of Patchen on cover
by Robin Carson.

3000 copies at $3.95 in first impression. Three additional printings of 3000 to
date; later printings indicated as such of verso of title-leaf.

Contents as (a)

A35   BUT EVEN SO   1968

a. *First Edition*

[Drawing] / BUT EVEN SO / KENNETH PATCHEN / A NEW DIRECTIONS BOOK

1 blank leaf, 4 leaves, [96] pp., 1 blank leaf. 21 x 14.5 cm. Yellow cloth with
black lettering and design. Grey, black, and white dust-wrapper with white
and black lettering.

Published on October 31 at $4.50. 2000 copies printed.

Contents: They Don't Seem To Understand—go Loving—This room, this
battlefield—Come now, my child—The Argument of Innocence—What
Walking Looks Like—The Hands of the Air—Ah, Come this Time—Quiet—
Can't Recall Me One Reason—King Jiz—Then Shall The Roads Arise—O
tonight the stars—A Gown of Clouds—Yeah, Jack, it's a dark deck—Caring—
The Daydream Of A Caterpillar—It Is Outside Us—What is not, then—Tigly
Kottaeau—At one time the grass was thought to be—And Mr Eggleg said—
My Name Is Dobble—Sure, Leroy—The Christ Who is here now—Peace now
for all men—Mr Plickpoon of Darby Doon—Gredgys Gookin—The Horse
Smile-Seller—The Rain Never Gets Wet—As bitter & bar as a tiger's frown—
His suchamuch?—A Mountain's Knees—O Fountain—Little Night-Eater
Knows—Oh, oh . . . "Bullet Eye" Brexton—It's outside The Thing That Dances
—My God the Sorrow of it—And Pocahontas She Done Cry—The Crimson

Leopard—How Do You Mourn Those Dead?—We Deserve Us—What Shall
We Do Without Us?—All That Leaves Is Here Always

b. *First Paperback Edition* (1968)

Title page as (a). Stiff paper wrappers.

6000 copies published at $1.50; two additional printings of 6000 to date; later
printings identified as such on verso of title-leaf.

Contents as (a)

A36   LOVE AND [i.e., &] WAR POEMS   1968

a. *First Edition, first issue*

[Cover acts as title-leaf] LOVE & WAR POEMS / [Biographical
blurb] / KENNETH PATCHEN / whisper & shout no. one 2s 6d
or 1 dollar [Mickleover, England: Whisper & Shout]

[1], 63 [1] pp. 21 x 15 cm. Yellow paper, black stiff paper wrappers with white
lettering.

Date, number of copies, and price unknown.

Contents: [About Patchen:] Love Song (for Miriam and Kenneth Patchen):
Anon:—Ten Leagues Beyond The Wide World's End Methinks Is No Journey:
Essay by Dennis Gould—A Reading for Kenneth Patchen: Essay by Susan
Margolis—[By Patchen:] for Miriam Patchen (Give You a Lantern)—Have
You Killed Your Man For Today—Creation—There Are Not Many Kingdoms
Left—Vines With Their—For Losing Her Love All Would I Profane—When
The Stones Burst Into Flames—And The Sweet Christs—from The Argument
To The Hunted City—I Know The Hair, Tissue, Skin & This Room Has Mys-
tery Like a Trance—Blake (an introduction to William Blake's book of engrav-
ings: JOB, New York, 1946)—The Hunted City: V—And When Freedom is
Achieved—She Had Concealed Him in a Deep Dark Cave—Some Little
Sayings and Observations—Nice Day for a Lynching—The New Being—Where
My Stag-Antlered Love Moves—And What With The Blunders—FLowers
Riding—While the Sun Still Spends His Fabulous Money—When All That
Changes Is the World—We Go Out Together Into The Staring Town—When
We Were Here Together—23rd Street Runs Into Heaven—[About Patchen:]
Postscript: Patchen: Man of Anger and Light: an Essay by Henry Miller—
Kenneth Patchen Reads With Jazz in Canada: Essay by Alan Neil—Publica-
tions and Criticisms

b. *First Edition, second issue*

As (a), but red paper wrappers with black lettering.

A37   SELECTED POEMS [U.K.]   1968

First Edition

SELECTED / POEMS / [Rule] / KENNETH / PATCHEN /
[Publisher's Device] / JONATHAN CAPE / THIRTY BEDFORD
SQUARE / LONDON

x, 13-191 pp. 22.5 x 15 cm. Blue cloth with gold lettering. Blue pictorial dust-
wrapper with white lettering.

Published at £2.75. Number of copies printed unknown. *On verso of title-leaf:*
"This selection First Published 1968."

Contents: Before The Brave (1936), When in the course of human events—We
mutually pledge to each other—An Invitation to the dance—The red woman—
Letter to the old men—Loyality is the life you are—Note for a diary—Country
excursion—Leaflet (one)—Leaflet (two)—Poem in the form of a letter: to
Lauro de Bosis—Joe Hill listens to the praying—Pinning the tail on the donkey
—*First Will & Testament* (1939), Behold, one of several little Christs—The
queer client and the forest-inn—The fox—Fall of the evening star—A revolutionary prayer—I never had any other desire so strong—Religion is that I love
you—To whom it may concern—Niobe—Fog—Elegy for the silent voices and
the joiners of everything—Autumn is the crows' time—Career for a child of
five—He was alone (as in reality) upon his humble bed—Peter's diary in Goodentown—On the south-west coast of Erehwemos stands a romantic little village
—Early in the morning—Poem—*The Dark Kingdom* (1942), The sea is awash
with roses—The village Tudda—Heaven and earth—For losing her love all
would I profane—We go out together into the staring town—As we are so
wonderfully done with each other—Virtue—How God was made—What
happened in the camps—*The Teeth Of The Lion* (1942), Do I not deal with
angels—O my love the pretty towns—Who holds a throned country—The
lions of fire shall have their hunting—*Cloth Of The Tempest* (1943), In shadings
of an obscure punishment—The shapes and intensities of this man, this Confucius—The destruction of Carthage—Anubis—The nervousnesses of memory
—When the stones burst into flame—The castles of Dealekori—The stars are
occupied—Measure the kings—Wonderfully life O wonderfully living heart—
Thinking rock—Not to disturb this gay gathering—The friend of heaven—The
unfulfilling brightnesses—Anna Karenina and the love-sick river—To say is
you love someone—May I ask you a question, Mr Youngstown sheet & tube?—
The knowledge of old towns—My coat is dirty—No honor may be had—And
when freedom is achieve . . .—The Poon-ril poem—O that Jesus-Boy—Enjoyment of women—O fill your sack with tiger cubs—Be music, night—The shape
of one enterprise—The colony of the sun—The dimensions of the morning—
Rest, heart of the tired world—*An Astonished Eye Looks Out Of The Air*
(1945), Credit to Paradise—*Pictures Of Life And Of Death* (1946), O my
dearest—Shadows and spring flowers—All the roses of the world—Fun in the
golden voice—Land of the neverending heart—*Red Wine And Yellow Hair*
(1949), Hovenweep—The lute in the attic—Old man—If a poem can be headed
—Summer storm by the sea—The orange bears—How Jimsey O'Roon and

Peter Stack . . .—Winter at the inn—Down in the lone valley—Do me that love—Red wine and yellow hair—*When We Were Here Together* (1952-7), And her look touching the air—Flowers to the house—Who walks there?— The magical mouse—An unexpected impasse—In the moonlight—O now the drenched land wakes—Autobiographical note—When we were here together— *The Famous Boating Party* (1954), Worn on the—Not many kingdoms left— The great sled-makers—Wanderers of the pale wood (1-12)—That night the— *Doubleheader* (1966), A letter to God (1943)

A38 AFLAME AND AFUN OF 1970
WALKING FACES

a. *First Edition, first issue*

AFLAME AND AFUN / OF WALKING FACES / FABLES AND DRAWINGS / BY / KENNETH PATCHEN / A NEW DIRECTIONS BOOK

87 pp. 21 x 14 cm. Stiff white paper with black and grey design and lettering. New Directions paperbook 292. Later issues identified as such on bottom of back cover.

Published in March at $1.50. 200 copies printed.

Contents: Identical to A21, adding Williams, Jonathan, "How Fables Tapped Along the Sunken Corridors," pp. 85-87.

b. *First Edition, second issue*

Title-leaf as (a)

1 blank leaf, 3 leaves, 87 pp., 1 blank leaf. 21 x 14 cm. Tan cloth with gold lettering. White dust-wrapper with black and grey design and lettering.

Published on March 30 at $5.00. Under 1000 copies printed.

Contents as (a)

A39 THERE'S LOVE ALL DAY 1970

First Edition

THERE'S LOVE / Poems by California's KENNETH PATCHEN / Selected by Dee Danner Barwick / Illustrated by Tom di Grazia / ALL DAY / Hallmark Editions

1 blank leaf, 3 leaves, 5-61 [1] pp., 1 blank leaf. 19.5 x 12 cm. Green, purple, blue, orange, brown and grey cloth with black lettering. Matching dust-wrapper.

Published at $2.50. Number of copies unknown.

Contents: All is Safe—As Frothing Wounds of Roses—As She Was Thus Alone in the Clear Moonlight—As We Are So Wonderfully Done With Each Other—Beautiful You Are—Be Music, Night—Country Excursion—Creation —Crossing on Staten Island Ferry—Fall of the Evening Star—Fog—For Losing Her Love All Would I Profane—Give You a Lantern—In the Moon-light—It Is the Hour—Lonesome Boy Blues—My Darling Troubles Heaven With Her Loveliness—O My Love the Pretty Towns—O She Is As Lovely-Often—O Sleeping Falls the Maiden Snow—O When I Take My Love Out Walking—Perhaps It Is Time—Poemscapes—Poems for Miriam—Prominent Couple Believed Permanently Stuck to Porch—Religion Is That I Love You— She Had Concealed Him in A Deep Dark Cave—She is the Prettiest of Crea-tures—The Bird-Queen—The Fox—The Great Birds—The Snow is Deep on the Ground—The Wonderful Sun!—There's a Train Leaving Soon—23rd Street Runs Into Heaven—We Go Out Together Into the Staring Town—What Splendid Birthdays—What There Is—When We Were Here Together

A40   WONDERINGS   1971

WONDERINGS / [Drawing] / KENNETH PATCHEN / A NEW DIRECTIONS BOOK

1 blank leaf, 3 leaves, [88] pp., 2 blank leaves. 21 x 14.5 cm. Green cloth with gold lettering. Grey dust-wrapper with cover drawing by author and black an white lettering.

Published on March 24 at $5.95. 100 copies printed. *On verso of title-leaf:* "First published clothbound and as ND Paperbook 320 in 1971."

Contents: But if your previous—Any who live—And it is true—To Whomever —The Great Fly Fleet—O honor the bird—Alllight Saving Time—Binding the quiet into chalky sheaves—In Back Of Every Really Thoughtful Chicken— Believe that apples could talk—What Indeed!—With one tiny stick—O "listen" is like an elephant—Keep It—The Broom of Bells—Since in The patient eye— Berfu's Ox—If You Can Lose Your Head—This is "The Animal That Walks Sitting Down"—What a Lovely Morning!—Are You There?—The Moment—I see again that Giraffe-of-Sofas—Let us rejoice—House on horseback—Garrity The Gambling Man—To "Run the Crown"—O Quietly the Sun-Man Sits—The words that speak up—Quick Thinker—The monument-maker is little fellow—From "The Teakettle Suggestion"—He bangs his wings on the table!—It's Always Too Soon Or Too Late—All are all things true—An Old Lady Named Amber Sam—Counsel for the Offense—The King of Logoona—Unless there are flowers—Which of us is not flesh?—Who are you?—It's Really Lousy Taste— Wait up here—Sleeper Under The Tree—The Question Is—Tiger Contem-plating A Cake—Why you running, pal?—Do you really think somebody will find us in time?—A Floating—Waiting at the bathhouse—Seems different now—Arrival of the mail order dog—There is no point saying anything—Glory never guesses—A Surprise For The Bagpipe-Player—None can leave where he's going—May all that have life be delivered—Everyman is me

b. *First Paperback Edition*

As (a) but stiff decorative wrappers. 21 x 14 cm.

4500 copies published at $1.25; one additional printing of 4500 to date, so identified on verso of title-leaf.

Contents as (a)

A41   TELL YOU THAT I LOVE YOU   1971

First Edition

Tell You That I Love You / Three Love Poems / by Kenneth Patchin / Illustrated by Fred Klemuchin / HALLMARK EDITIONS

[52] pp. 15.5 x 10.5 cm. Pink, blue, and green cloth with black lettering. Pictorial dust-wrapper with black lettering.

No publication data.

Contents: Give You a Lantern—What There is in This My Green World—We Go Out Together Into the Staring Town

A42   IN QUEST OF CANDLELIGHTERS   1972

a. *First Edition*

IN QUEST OF / CANDLELIGHTERS / KENNETH PATCHEN / A NEW DIRECTIONS BOOK

1 blank leaf, 4 leaves, 3-137 pp., 1 blank leaf. 21 x 14 cm. Black cloth with gold lettering. White and black dust-wrapper with grey and black lettering.

Published on April 20 at $6.95. 1000 copies printed. *On verso of title-leaf:* "First published clothbound and as New Directions Paperbook 334 in 1972."

Contents: Panels for the Walls of Heaven—Angel-Carver Blues—Bury Them in God—They Keep Riding Down All The Time

b. *First Paperback Edition* (1972)

As (a) but stiff decorative wrappers.

5000 published.

A43   PATCHEN'S LOST PLAYS   1977

a. *First edition, regular issue*

PATCHEN'S / LOST PLAYS / DON'T LOOK NOW and / THE CITY WEARS A SLOUCH HAT / by Kenneth Patchen / edited and with an introduction by / Richard G. Morgan / [portrait of Patchen] / A NOEL YOUNG BOOK / Published by Capra Press, Santa Barbara / 1977

93 [1] pp., 1 leaf. 21.25 x 14 cm. Red, white, and black stiff wraps.

Published in October at $3.95; 5000 copies printed.

Contents: On the Side of the Angels [introduction, by Richad G. Morgan]— Don't Look Now—The City Wears a Slouch Hat

b. *First edition, limited issue*

Title page, pagination as (a). 22 x 14.25 cm. Red cloth with black lettering. Numbered and signed by editor.

Published in November at $10.00; 100 copies printed. *Colophon:* "Designed by Marcia Butt for Capra Press in Santa Barbara October 1977. Typeset by Charlene McAdams, printed by Haagen Printing and bound by Aaron Young. One hundred copies, numbered and signed by the editor, were handbound by Emily Paine."

Contents as (a)

B1 CHRISTMAS 1944 1944

'HOW SILENT ARE THE THINGS OF HEAVEN' [Bill Shank]

Broadside. 28 x 21 cm. Brown paper with black lettering.

Publication data unknown. Distributed gratis by Bill Shank as a Christmas Greeting.

B2 WHAT IS THE BEAUTIFUL? 1947

WHAT IS THE BEAUTIFUL / [decorative device] / [text of poem] [Rosemont, PA: The Ahab Press]

Folio. Single sheet, 18.5 x 23 cm, folded once to 18.5 x 11.5 cm. Cream-colored paper.

About two dozen printed and distributed gratis as Christmas greetings by a friend of Patchen.

B3 JUST OUTSIDE TOMSTONE 1957

[Within light red block.] JUST OUTSIDE / TOMBSTONE / [Below block:]A POEM BY KENNETH PATCHEN / [Thick black rule] [Hennypenny Press]

Folio. One sheet 48 x 31 cm., folded twice to form a 24 x 15.5 cm folio. Heavy cream-color paper; deckled edge.

Printed in September. Number of copies unknown, but quite limited. Distributed gratis. *On back: "Just Outside Tombstone* appeared in *Miscellaneous Man* Number 10 and is reprinted by permission. This folio has been designed and printed by Robert Greenwood at the Talisman Press for the Hennypenny Press."

B4 TWO POEMS FOR CHRISTMAS 1958

[In red:] TWO POEMS FOR CHRISTMAS / [In black:] BY KENNETH PATCHEN [Palo Alto, California: Kenneth Patchen]

Folio. Single sheet 20 x 41.5 cm. [copies vary slightly], folded in two places to 20 x 14 cm. Paper. Colors vary, primarily off-white; a few copies were gray.

200 copies printed in December and distributed gratis. *On back*: "Handset in Baskerville types and printed by John Hunter Thomas on rag papers of the last century which were used in the preservation of botanical specimens."

Contents: I Have Lighted the Candles, Mary—Nothing Has Changed

B5   SMALL POST CARDS   1958

Set of four, a Christmas present from Kenneth to Miriam Patchen. 15 x 10 cm. 500 of each card printed.

a. "In Perkko's Grotto"

a. "It Is Somehow Reassuring"

c. "The Walker Standing"

d. "The One"

B6   I HAVE LIGHTED THE CANDLES, MARY   1958

[In red:] I HAVE LIGHTED / THE CANDLES, MARY [Palo Alto, California: Kenneth Patchen]

Folio. Single sheet 23.5 x 31 cm. folded once to 23.5 x 15.5 cm. Heavy white paper with red and black lettering. Poem is printed on front; rest of folio blank.

250 copies printed in December. Distributed gratis.

B7   A POEM FOR XMAS   1960

(In red:] A POEM FOR XMAS / [In black:] BY KENNETH PATCHEN [Palo Alto, California: Kenneth Patchen

Folio. Single sheet 18 x 26 cm., folded once to 18 x 13 cm. White rag paper; red and black printing.

200 copies printed in December. Distributed gratis. *On back*: "Handset in Baskerville Types and printed by John H. Thomas."

Contents: To Give Us Each A Love

B8   PATCHEN CARDS   1962

Fourteen different letterpaper cards and envelopes issued by the Patchens in two set of seven, labelled "Picture-Poems by Kenneth Patchen," and sold by them for $1.50 per set. 20 x 12.5 cm. 500 of each card printed. Each is a first appearance in print. All were later printed in *Hallelujah Anyway* (A34).

a. *Series R*
  1. No. 121. "Peace or Perish"
  2. No. 122. "Now Is Then's Only Tomorrow"
  3. No. 123. "Unless You Clock In"
  4. No. 124. "Upon the book of the waters"
  5. No. 125. "Tree-Sleeping Behind Lectures"
  6. No. 126. "Check! Questions Are The Best Things I Answer, Bub"
  7. No. 127. "The Walking-Away World"

b. *Series RS*
  1. No. 221. "Oh Come Now! There Is A Beautiful Place!"
  2. No. 222, "Peace or we all perish"
  3. No. 223. "There Isn't Much More To Tell"
  4. No. 224. "You Know, Somehow I Think, Old Pal"
  5. No. 225. "Man Is Not A Town"
  6. No. 226. "All Right, You May Alight"
  7. No. 227. "Now, When I Get Back Here"

B9 PEACE AND GOOD WILL 1962

[Holograph, all within decorative border:] PEACE / AND / GOOD / WILL / 1962 [Palo Alto, California: Kenneth Patchen]

Folio. Single sheet 37.5 x 23.5 cm., folded twice to 18.5 x 11.5 cm. Off-white, hand-painted and lettered in various colors. Lettering on front, design inside.

Only a few were made; exact number unknown. Distributed gratis.

B10 A POEM FOR CHRISTMAS 1963

[In red:] A POEM FOR CHRISTMAS 1963 / BY KENNETH PATCHEN [Palo Alto, California: Kenneth Patchen]

Folio. 18 x 13 cm. Stiff white paper.

250 copies printed in December. Distributed gratis.

Contents: Peace on Earth

B11 SEASON'S GREETINGS 1963

SEASON'S / GREET- / INGS [Palo Alto, California: Kenneth Patchen]

Folio. Single sheet 31 x 23.5 cm., folded twice to 15.5 x 12 cm. Stiff white paper.

250 copies printed in December. Distributed gratis.

Contents: Dear Friends—Peace or Perish

B12   A PARABLE AT YEAR'S END   1964

A PARABLE AT YEAR'S END [Palo Alto, California: Kenneth Patchen]

Folio. 10 x 14.5 cm. White paper. Drawing on front, poem inside.

250 copies printed. Distributed gratis.

B13   BEFORE THE BELLS OF   1967
                 THIS NEW YEAR RING

[In red:] 1967 / BEFORE THE BELLS OF / THIS NEW YEAR RING [Palo Alto, California: Kenneth Patchen]

Broadside. 31 x 23.5 cm. Stiff off-white paper, bottom edge untrimmed.

250 copies printed. Distributed gratis. *At bottom of page:* "from *First Will and Testament* (revised)."

B14   TOBIN CARDS   1968

Twelve different cards, produced individually, each titled "A Patchen Picture-Poem" on back of card. White paper board, 20 x 13.5 cm. Only a few hundred cards were actually printed, before Tobin's company was disbanded.

a. "Hallelujah"
b. "I Am The Ghost of Chief Mountain Lyin' "
c. "Of Course They Will Win"
d. "Imagine Seeing You Here"
e. "Peace Or We Will All Perish"
f. "Peace or Perish"
g. "Little Chief Son-of-a-Gun"
h. "What Can You Do Up Here"
i. "The Best Hope"
j. "I Have a Funny Feeling"
k. "I Proclaim This International"
l. "The One"

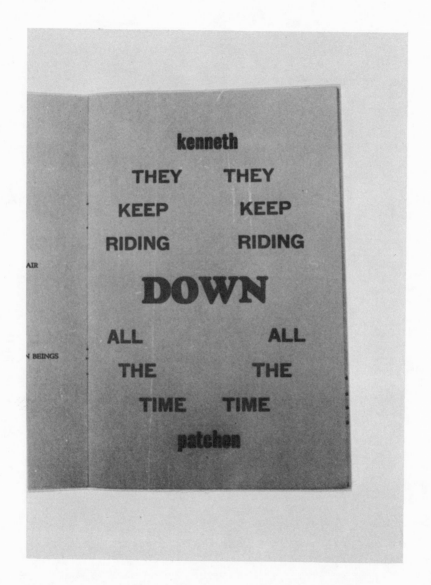

Title Page of *They Keep Riding Down All the Time* (1946-7). A14.

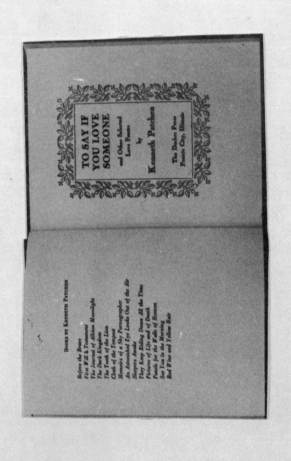

TO SAY IF
YOU LOVE
SOMEONE

and Other Selected
Love Poems

by

Kenneth Patchen

The Decker Press
Prairie City, Illinois

Title Page of *To Say If You Love Someone* (1948). A17b.

B15 UNTITLED DRAWINGS 1968

Series of four, packaged together, reprinted from *Whisper & Shout* (England). 12 x 15.5 cm. *On back:* "Untitled Drawing. First U.S. printing: reproduced by special permission of Kenneth Patchen. Originally published in *Love & War Poems* by Whisper and Shout, Derby England, February 1968."

B16 NOTHING HAS CHANGED 1970

NOTHING HAS CHANGED [Mountain View, CA: The Artichoke Press]

Broadside. 43 x 26.5 cm. enclosed in wrapper and printed envelope. Individually hand-colored by Patchen.

Published in December at $40.00. Thirty copies printed, half reserved for private distribution. Printed on 18th century rag paper.

B17 BELIEVE THAT APPLES COULD TALK 1974

Card. 16.5 x 13 cm. Publication data unknown.

Produced in connection with the exhibition, "The Works of Kenneth Patchen," at the University Art Galley, University of North Dakota, March 18-April 5, 1974.

B18 A GREETING IN MERCY 1976

KENNETH PATCHEN / A POEM FOR CHRISTMAS / ARTICHOKE MCMLXXVI [Mountain View, California: The Artichoke Press]

Folio. Single sheet 37 x 26.5 cm. Screen-printed in gold and maroon on handsome paper tipped into green folder with red and blue lettering measuring 38.5 x 28 cm. Signed by printer and Miriam Patchen.

Published in December at $40.00. 100 copies printed.

SECTION C
CONTRIBUTIONS TO BOOKS AND PAMPHLETS

C1   THE POETS SPEAK   1943

THE POETS SPEAK / TWELVE POEMS FROM A SERIES
OF READINGS AT / THE NEW YORK PUBLIC LIBRARY /
OCTOBER AND NOVEMBER, 1943 / WITH AN INTRODUC-
TION BY / MAY SARTON / [device] / NEW YORK / THE
NEW YORK PUBLIC LIBRARY / 1943

22 pp. 22 x 18 cm. Light blue paper with black lettering.

Contains "What Is The Beautiful?" on page 17.

C2   THE HAPPY ROCK   1945

THE HAPPY ROCK / [Line drawing of Henry Miller] / A /
BOOK / ABOUT / HENRY MILLER [Berkeley, California: Bern
Porter]

2 blank leaves, 1 leaf, 1 blank leaf, 4 leaves, 1-157 [1] pp., 3 blank leaves. Tan
paper boards with red and black lettering.

On verso of title-leaf: "Of the three thousand copies printed for Bern Porter
by the Packard Press at Berkeley, seven hundred and fifty were bound for
distribution during 1945."

Contains "Tribute and Protest" on page 124.

C3   PATCHEN: MAN OF ANGER AND LIGHT   1946

[Beginning at left margin, and extending 3/4 into black-bordered
rectangle, in red:] PATCHEN: MAN OF ANGER & LIGHT BY
HENRY MILLER / [Below, beginning 1/2 inside red-bordered
rectangle, and extending to right margin, in black:] A LETTER
TO GOD BY KENNETH PATCHEN [New York: Padell]

32 pp. 23.5 x 15.5 cm. Pictorial paper cover, reading PATCHEN / MAN OF
ANGER & LIGHT / BY HENRY MILLER.

Published at $1.00. 2500 copies printed. *On verso of title-leaf:* "(A Letter to God
was first published in *Retort*)."

Contains "A Letter to God."

C4   JOB   1947

a. *First Edition, first issue*

JOB / INVENTED & ENGRAVED / [device] BY / WILLIAM / BLAKE / INTRODUCTORY NOTE BY KENNETH PATCHEN / UNITED BOOK GUILD NEW YORK

24 leaves. Unbound in portfolio measuring 41 x 27 cm. Black cloth and linen with grey and white design and lettering.

Patchen's introduction comprises both sides of the first sheet.

b. *Second Edition*

As (a), but bound. Same size, materials, and design as portfolio.

C5   SPEARHEAD   1947

SPEARHEAD / 10 YEARS' EXPERIMENTAL / WRITING IN AMERICA / A NEW DIRECTIONS BOOK [Parsippany, N.J.: New Directions]

604 pp. 23 x 16 cm. Beige cloth with white lettering. Grey, black and yellow dust-wrapper with white and black lettering.

Contains "Six Poems: The Character of Love; The Poor Child With the Hooked Hands; Do the Dead Know What Time It Is?; O My Darling Troubles Heaven With Her Loveliness; He Was Alone," and "House of the Frowning Heart," a chapter from near the end of *Memoirs of a Shy Pornographer,* all on pages 367-88.

SECTION D
CONTRIBUTIONS TO PERIODICALS

1928

D 1. "The Christ of the Andes." *High School Life* IX, 8 (April 12, 1928) 4. Poem. This was the student publication of Warren G. Harding High School in Warren, Ohio, which Patchen attended from 1926 to 1929. He was on the staff of the publication in 1928.

D 2. "Plea of the Insane." *High School Life* IX, 11 (May 18, 1928) 2. Poem.

D 3. "Have Mercy." *High School Life* X, 1 (October 22, 1928) 4. Poem.

D 4. "To Alan Seager." *High School Life* X, 3 (November 23, 1928) 5. Poem.

1929

D 5. "Aspiration." *High School Life* X, 9 (May 10, 1929) 8. Poem.

D 6. "Improbable Realities." *High School Life* X, 11 (May 24, 1929) 5. Poem.

1932

D 7. "Permanence." *New York Times* (April 10, 1932) Section 3, 1. Poem. Though another poem of Patchen's is mentioned as having appeared several years earlier in the *Times*, I have been able to find no record of it.

D 8. "Reversing the Inquest." *The Rebel Poet*, no.14 (July 1932) 4. Poem.

D 9. "Lenin." *The Rebel Poet*, no. 17 (October 1932) 5. Poem.

1934

D 10. "Three Poems: Empty Dwelling Places, Tristanesque, Parting Coney Island." *Poetry* XLIII (January 1934) 190-192.

D 11. "When the Snow Melts in Siberia." *Poems for a Dime*, no. 1 (June 17, 1934) n.p. Poem.

D 12. "Gilding for Dreams." *New Republic* LXXIX, 1025 (July 25, 1934) 298. Review of Christopher La Farge, *Hoxie Sells His Acres*.

D 13.   "My Generation Reading the Newspapers." *The Maga-zine: A Journal of Contemporary Writing* II, 1 (July-August 1934) 11. Poem.

D 14.   "Three Poems: The Red Woman, Creed, Poem." *Poems for a Dime*, no. 3 (November 7, 1934) n.p.

D 15.   "Joe Hill Listens to the Praying." *New Masses* XVI (November 20, 1934) 8-9. Poem.

D 16.   "Poem in the Form of a Letter: To Lauro de Bosis." *The Magazine: A Journal of Contemporary Writing* II, 3 (November-December 1934) 141-144.

1935

D 17.   "For Edgar A. Poe." *Canadian Forum* XV (January 1935) 148. Poem.

D 18.   "Leighton Brewer, *Riders of the Sky*." *New Republic* LXXXI, 1053 (February 6, 1935) 369. Book review.

D 19.   "Loneliness." *Canadian Forum* XV (March 1935) 228. Poem.

D 20.   "The Pilgrim Bark." *Harper's Magazine* CLXX (March 1935) 417. Poem.

D 21.   "The Ladder." *Trend* III, 1 (March-April, 1935) 28. Poem.

D 22.   "Robert Faherty, *Better Than Dying*." *New Republic* LXXXIV, 1090 (October 23, 1935) 314-315. Book review.

1936

D 23.   "Letter to the Young Men." *American Prefaces* I, 4 (January 1936) 64. Poem.

D 24.   "Mill Strike." *New Republic* LXXXV, 1105 (February 5, 1936) 365. Poem.

D 25.   "Let Us Have Madness." *Literary Digest* CXXII (September 5, 1936) 28. Poem.

D 26.   "The Fox." *Saturday Review of Literature* XIV, 23 (October 3, 1936) 4. Poem.

D 27.   "I Knew a Man Who Loved That Germany," "Camping Out on the Mountain," "To the Heroes to Make Much of the Millionaire's Death." *Signatures: Work in Progress*, no. 2 (Autumn 1936) 231-232. Poems.

D 28.   "Creation." *Smoke* V, 3 (Autumn 1936) 26. Poem.

D 29.   "The Deer and the Snake." *Saturday Review of Literature* XV, 5 (November 28, 1936) 6. Poem.

D 30. "Forest Camp." *Poems for a Dime*, no. 5 (November 1936) n.p. Poem.

1937

D 31. "The Plain of Cooldrevin." *The Household Magazine* (May 1937) 8-9. Short story.

D 32. "The Hound Who Saved the Enemy." *Fantasy* V, 4 (1937) 15. Prose-poem.

1938

D 33. "The Poor Thing Crying at Night." *Partisan Review* IV, 3 (February 1938) 18-19. Poem.

D 34. "Religion is That I Love You." *New Mexico Sentinel* II, 30 (July 3, 1938) 10. Poem.

D 35. "Lights Are Going Out in the Castles: Hymn to a Trench Gun; Boxers Hit Harder When Women Are Around; Inasmuch as War Is Not for Women." *Voices*, no. 94 (Summer 1938) 20-21. Poems.

D 36. "Autumn is the Crow's Time." *New Republic* XCVI, 1241 (September 14, 1938) 156. Poem.

D 37. "Two Fragments from 'Peter's Diary in Goodentown'." *Twice-a-Year*, no. 1 (Fall-Winter 1938) 190. Poems.

D 38. "Can the Harp Shoot Through Its Propellers?" *New Directions in Prose and Poetry* no. 3 (1938) 128. Poem.

D 39. "The Swimmer." *Fantasy* VI, 1 (1938) 14. Poem.

1939

D 40. "The Fox." *Voice of Scotland* I, 3 (December 1938-February 1939) 22. Poem.

D 41. "Street Corner College." *American Mercury* XLVI (April 1939) 491-492. Poem.

D 42. "Christmas on Lake Michigan." *Compass* I, 1 (Winter 1939) n.p. Poem.

D 43. "Crossing on Staten Island Ferry." *Voices*, no. 97 (Spring 1939) 27. Poem.

D 47. "So When She Lay Beside Me." *Poetry* LV (November 1939) 71. Poem.

D 45. "Hymn to a Railroad Lick." *Compass* I, 2 (Spring 1939) n.p. Poem. Includes a note on Patchen.

D 46. "Seven Poems About the Way to Go Out of the World: Stayed No Longer in the Place Than to Hire a Guide for the Next Stage; I Suddenly Became Conscious That the Thing Was Looking at Me Intently; He Thought of Mad Ellen's Ravings, and of the Wretched Skeleton on the Rock; How Different the Expressions of This Face!; The Figure Motioned With Its Mangled Hand Towards the Wall Behind It, and Uttered a Melancholy Cry; The Queer Client and the Forest Inn; Behold One of Several Little Christs," "Four Poems About What the Hand-writing on the Walls Says: The Overworld; Elegy For the Silent Voices and the Joiners of Everything; Fifth Dimension; All the Bright Foam of Talk." *Fantasy* VI, 2 (1939) 15-20, 23-25.

D 47. "Bury Them in God," "On the South West Coast of Erehwemos," "Man is to Man a Beast." *New Directions in Prose and Poetry*, no. 4 (1939) 128-150. First selection is prose, the other two are poems.

D 48. "These Have Gone With Silent Hands Seeking," "from Argument (The Hunted City)." *Twice-a-Year* nos. 3-4 1939-1940) 286-295. First selection is a poem, the second is part of a prose-poem.

1940

D 49. "The Letter to the Young Men: II." *American Prefaces: A Journal of Critical and Imaginative Writings.* V, 9 (June 1940) 143. Poem.

D 50. "History in a Minor Key," "Don't Wash Your Hair in the Street car, Nora," "So It Ends." "Vinegar and Perfume," "Christ, Christ, Christ, That the World," "The State of the Nation." *Contour* no. 2 (November 1940) 38-43. Poems.

1941

D 51. "A Bit of Something for Somebody," "A Letter to Albion Moonlight." *Now* I, 1 (August 1941) 30. First is a poem, the second prose.

D 52. "14 Poems: The Death Givers; The Crowded Net; Waking Into Sleep; How To Be Happy; The Intimate Guest; A Temple; ABCDEFQRXYG; The Priestess; The Meaning of Life; The Spirit of the Place; The Naked

Land; Digging for Clams; A Devotion; Hill Sky," "Poem: Sometimes My Inclination Lay in Another Direction," "From the Notebook of St. Donna," "A Fragment From the Diary of a Monster." *Experimental Review* I, 3 (September 1941) 1-17. Includes a note on Patchen.

D 53.   "We're All Fools." *Story* XVII (September-October 1941) 87. Poem.

1942

D 54.   "We Go Out Together into the Staring Town." *Harper's Bazaar* (February 1942) 92. Poem.

D 55.   "Poemes Americains Traduits par Ivan Goll: Le Roi de Tenebres, Qui Possede un Royal Domaine." *La Voix de France* (August 15, 1942) 9. Poems.

D 56.   "Unfulfilling Brightnesses." *Saturday Review of Literature* XXV, 45 (November 7, 1942) 10. Poem.

D 57.   "To the Makers," "The Lions of Fire Shall Have Their Hunting." *Retort* I, 3 (December 1942) 24-25. Poems.

D 58.   "Whitman, 'our all-aroundest poet,' is culled by Mark Van Doren." *The Knoxville News-Sentinel* (December 20, 1942) 15. Review of *The Portable Walt Whitman.*

D 59.   "I Have Lighted the Candles, Mary." *Herald Tribune Books* (December 20, 1942) 1. Poem.

D 60.   "I Have Lighted the Candles, Mary." *Knoxville News-Sentinel* (December 20, 1942) 1. Poem.

D 61.   "Six Poems: How God Was Made; Virtue; For Losing Her All Would I Profane; About Water and the World's End; The Wolf of Winter; This is the Beginning." *Fantasy*, no. 26 (1942) 3-6.

1943

D 62.   "The Temple of Diana," "The Battle of Hasan." *Partisan Review* X, 1 (January-February 1943) 59-60. Poems.

D 63.   "Egypt." *Poetry* LXI (March 1943) 667. Poem.

D 64.   "Instructions for Angels," "To the German People." *Retort* I, 4 (Spring 1943) 27-28. Poems.

D 65.   "Je Separa la vue de la Chose Vue," "La Porte de Salut est Large Sur le Village Qui Glisse a Travers le Soleil." Trans. Jean Wahl. *Fontaine: Ecrivains et Poetes de Etats-Unis D' Amerique* [France], nos. 27-28 (July 1943) 205. Poems.

D 66. "Three Poems: The Creation of America; The Destruction of Carthage; The Unnatural History of Peru." *Hemispheres*, no. 1 (Summer 1943) 30-32. French-American.

D 67. "A Letter to God." *Retort* II, 1 (November 1943) 24-33. Prose.

D 68. "The Age of Pericles." *Chimera* II, 2 (Autumn 1943) 2. Poem.

D 69. "Regarding the Nature and Accomplishments of Heaven." *New Directions in Prose and Poetry*, no. 8 (1943) 134-139. Poem.

D 70. " 'In Horror the God-Thrown Lie,' " "The Carriage," " 'At the Cave,' " " 'Hold thy Tongue, Death,' " " 'For Whose Adornment' " " 'Of the Same Beauty Were Stars Made,' " "When Will the Water Come In?" "Sustainer of Clay Blessings," "Work for Mountains," "When the Beautiful Wakes," "Luda," " 'In Thy Falling Have Flame,' " "Flourish in Thy Season," " 'The Ancient Whim of Man's Will,' " "Choice of Forms," " 'What Name, Light?' " "The Lively Enchanters," " 'He Feeds on All,' " "Chatter," " 'No Honor May Be Had,' " "Thanksgiving," " 'And by Finding This One Earth,' " " 'Attempt It in Fear,' " " 'The Mule of Water,' " " 'The Taste of Wood,' " "Childhood," " 'Cloud Drone Boot Rattle,' " "Nainda," " 'Fill the Mountain,' " "November in Ohio," "Shadows Kiss the Garden," "The Cold," "Happiness of the Mother," "The Friend of Heaven," "Death and Luda As Contending." *Fantasy*, no. 27 (1943) 3-10. Poems.

1944

D 71. " 'Be Music, Night.' " *New York Times Book Review* (February 20, 1944) 2. Poem.

D 72. "How Silent Are the Things of Heaven." *New York Times Book Review* (March 19, 1944) 2. Poem.

D 73. "Two Poems about Heaven and Earth: Where That Gate and That Throne; I Suppose You Wonder What Death Is and What Life Is." *Harper's Bazaar* (March 1944) 144.

D 74. "The Dazzling Burden," "Joined Together By The Rule of Peaceful Love," "I Feel Drunk All the Time." *Prairie Schooner* XVIII, 4 (Winter 1944) 252-253. Poems.

D 75. "I Suppose You Wonder What Death Is and What Life Is." *Maryland Quarterly*, no. 1 (1944) 10. Poem.

D 76. "Sleepers Awake on the Precipice." *New Directions in Prose and Poetry*, no. 9 (1944) 191-212. Prose. First chapter of the novel.

D 77. "The Landscapes of Paradise," "Figures of Speech," "The Lean Ones of God are Clothed in Victories," "Sport of Dazzling Princes." *Circle* I, 3 (1944) 9-11. Poems. Includes note on Patchen.

D 78. "Reflections on the Journal of Albion Moonlight." *Transformation*, no. 4 (1944) 214-216. Prose.

D 79. "Three poems: How Silent are the things of Heaven; The Appian Way; The Destruction of Carthage." *The Windmill* I (1944) 89-90.

1945

D 80. "Credit to Paradise." *Briarcliff Quarterly* I, 4 (January 1945) 215. Poem.

D 81. "Poems Which are Written By the Soul." "The Stars Go to Sleep So Peacefully." *The Harvard Wake* I (June 1945) 9-10. Poems.

D 82. "I Always Return to This Place." *University of Kansas Review* XI, 3 (Spring 1945) 184. Poem.

D 83. "Science Talked," "I Feel Drunk All the Time," "The Stars Go to Sleep So Peacefully," *The Illiterati*, no. 4 (Summer 1945) 1-2. Poems.

D 84. "The First Chapter of Kenneth Patchen's New Book." *P.M.* (September 1945) 12ff. First chapter of *Memoirs of a Shy Pornographer.*

D 85. "Sleepers Awake on the Precipice." *Retort* III, 1 (Fall 1945) 9-19. Prose. Section of *Sleepers Awake.*

D 86. "Ezra Pound's Guilt." *Conscientious Objector* (December 1945) 4. Essay on Pound.

D 87. "The King of Cold." *Gangrel*, no. 3 (1945) 31. Poem.

D 88. "Do the Dead Know What Time is is?" *Modern Reading*, no. 13 (1945) 90. Poem.

1946

D 89. "A Statement by the Author." [Prose statement about an essay by David Gascoyne in the same issue]; "Three Early Poems: The Sea Has Caves and Urns; Geography of Music; At the New Year," "O Fiery River," "Rest, Heart of the Tired World." *Poetry Quarterly* VIII, 1 (Spring 1946) 10, 11-14.

D 90. "I Have Lighted the Candles." *Community News* I, 13 (December 22, 1946) 3. Poem.

D 91. "Sleepers Awake." *Circle* nos. 7-8 (1946) 28-36. Prose. Section of *Sleepers Awake.*

1947

D 92. "Every Time a Door Opens Somebody's Heart Gets Busted." *Mademoiselle* (March 1947) 188-189, 319, 320-327. Prose. Section of *Sleepers Awake.*

D 93. "Sez Henry Miller." *Saturday Review of Literature* XXX, 15 (April 12, 1947) 36. Letter.

D 94. "Sleepers Awake." *The Ark*, no. 1 (Spring 1947) 5-11. Prose. Section of *Sleepers Awake.*

D 95. "Five Poems: History in a Minor Key; So It Ends; Vinegar and Perfume; Christ! Christ! Christ! That the World; The State of the Nation." *Contour Quarterly*, no. 2 (September 1947) 38-43.

D 96. "Beings So Hideous," "The Stars Go To Sleep So Peacefully," "Summer Day." *Poetry Quarterly* IX, 3 (Autumn 1947) 159-161. Poems.

1948

D 97. "As Frothing Wounds of Roses." *The Tiger's Eye* I, 3 (March 15, 1948) 2. Poem.

D 98. "See You in the Morning." *Woman's Home Companion* LXXV (March 1948) 18ff. Prose. Condensed version of the book.

D 99. "A Song of Crucifixion." *Neurotica* I, 1 (Spring 1948) 23. Poem.

D100. "This Summer Earth." *New Quarterly of Poetry* II, 4 (Summer 1948) 3. Poem.

D101. "Poor Gorrel. *The Bridge* II, 10 (July 20, 1948) 152-153. Poem.

D102. "Wouldn't You Be After a Jaunt of 964,000,000,000,000 Miles?" "All You Can Ever Do is Let it Rain." *The Bridge* III, 1 (September 7, 1948) 6-8. Poems.

D103. "This Summer Earth." *New York Herald Tribune* (October 3, 1948) 11. Poem.

D104. "Lament for the Makers." *Epoch: A Quarterly of Contemporary Literature* II, 1 (Fall 1948) 60. Poem.

D105. "Fog Over the Sea and the Sun Going Down." *Western Review* XIII, 1 (Autumn 1948) 16. Poem.

D106. "The New Being." *Neurotica* I, 2 (Autumn 1948) 53-54.
       Poem.

D107. "Two Poems About Heaven and Earth." *The Tiger's
       Eye* I, 6 (December 15, 1948) 14.

D108. "Statement." *The Flying Fish* (1948) inside front cover.
       Prose. Information on *Sleepers Awake* and *The Journal
       of Albion Moonlight*.

D109. "Do Me That Love," "The Lute in the Attic." *Contem-
       porary Poetry* VIII, 3 (1948) 10-12. Poems.

D110. "The Event at Konna." *Prairie Schooner* XXII (1948)
       272. Poem.

D111. "The Little Black Train." *Golden Goose*, no. 2 (1948)
       24-25. Poem.

D112. "Mr. Barker's Fat Lady." *Golden Goose*, no. 3 (1948)
       32-33. Poem.

D113. "The Orange Bears." *New Mexico Quarterly Review*
       XVIII, 4 (1948) 392. Poem.

D114. "Poor Gorrel," "All You Ever Do is Let it Rain." *The
       Bridge (Supplement)*, no. 1 (1948) 6-7. Poems.

D115. "The Radiance in a Dark Wood," "Two for History,"
       "A Lost Poem." *Quarterly Review of Literature* IV, 3
       (1948) 245-247. Poems.

D116. "To Bunneni, Hake and Clem Maugre, the Seers of Gloc-
       cus—As well as to all other forgotten minstrels of our
       enlightenment." *Interim* III, 3 (1948) 19. Poem.

D117. "The Value of Caution for This Journey." *Berkeley: A
       Journal of Modern Culture*, no. 5 (1948) 5. Poem.

D118. "The Little Black Train." *The Wind and the Rain* V, 3
       (Winter, 1948-1949) n.p. Poem.

1949

D119. "Relieving the Tension of the Troops," "A Bunch of
       Flowers." *Gale* I, 1 (April 1949) 5. Poems.

D120. "A Bibliography." *The Bridge* III, 12 (April 15, 1949)
       263-267. Patchen's own listing of his books, for a bibli-
       ography of poets who appeared in *The Bridge Supple-
       ment* in 1948.

D121. "La Renarde," "Christ! Christ! Christ! Que Le Monde,"
       "Les Etoiles S'en Vont Dormir Si Paisiblement," "Pan-
       neau Quarante Quatre" (from *Panels*). *Le Journal des
       Poetes* [France], no. 5 (June 1949) 4. Poems; also biog-
       raphy by M. Carlier, criticism by Pierre Lesdain.

D122. "Two Poems: A Plate of Steaming Fish; The Lute in the Attic." *Poetry Ireland (An American Issue)*, no. 7 (October 1949) 14-16.

D123. "Fun in The Golden Voice." *Delphic Review* I, 1 (Winter 1949) 33. Poem. Includes note on Patchen.

D124. "The Hunter." *Golden Goose*, no. 4 (1949) 20. Poem.

D125. "And a Man Went Out Alone." *Golden Goose* [Chapbook Series], no. 6 (Autumn 1949) 8. Poem.

D126. "If a Poem Can be Headed Into Its Proper Current Someone Will Take it Within His Heart to the Power and Beauty of Everybody." *Approach*, no. 5 (1949) 2-3. Poem.

D127. "Old Man." *Zero* I (1949) 18. Poem.

D128. "A Pile of Rusty Beer Cans," "Family Portrait." *Contour*, no. 4 (1949) 43-44. First Selection is poetry, the second a prose-poem.

1950

D129. "The Role of Ideas in Fiction." *Occident* (Spring 1950) 9-10. Prose.

D130. "If a Poem Can Be Headed," "Aspiration." *Cauldron* L, 1 (December 1950) 13-15. Poems. Anniversary edition of the literary magazine of Warren G. Harding High School, Warren, Ohio, where Patchen was a student. Includes note on Patchen.

1951

D131. "Symposium on Writing." *Golden Goose* [new series] III, 2 (Autumn 1951) 89-96. Patchen was among the writers who participated in the symposium; the others were William Carlos Williams, Charles Olson, Henry Rago, and Leslie Woolf Hedley.

D132. "Here Was the Bride Ready." *Inferno* no. 2 (1951) 5. Poem.

1952

D133. "Irkalla's White Caves." *Perspectiven*, no. 1 (October 1952) 174-177. Poem. German-English.

D134. "But of Life?" *Poetry* LXXXI (October 1952) 61. Poem.

D135. "A-Berrying We Will Go." *Golden Goose* [new series] III, 3 (1952) 140. Prose-poem.

1953

D136.   "Four Poems: Beatiful You Are; The Unanswering Corre-
         spondences; All Is Safe; Under a Tree." *Poetry* 82
         (April 1953) 23-26.
D137.   "Poemscapes." *New Directions in Prose and Poetry*, no. 14
         (1953) 262-264. Prose-poems.

1954

D138.   "Qui Possede un Royal Domaine." *Le Journal Des Poetes*
         [France] XXIV, 6 (June 1954) 8. Poem. Also biograph-
         ical note.
D139.   "Sette poesie d'amore: As She Was Thus Alone in the
         Clear Moonlight; The Snow is Deep on the Ground;
         The Fall of the Evening Star; The Character of Love
         Seen As a Search For the Lost; For Whose Adornment;
         Of the Same Beauty Were Stars Made; Be Music,
         Night." *Prospette* [Italy], no. 8 (1954) 138-147. Poems
         in English, with Italian translations.

1955

D140.   "Wide, Wide in the Rose's Side." "O She is as Lovely-
         Often," "The Great Birds," "First Came the Lion-Rider,"
         "O Now the Drenched Land Wakes." *Poetry* LXXXVI
         (May 1955), 71-73. Poems.

1956

D141.   "Some Little Sayings and Observations." *Liberation* I,
         1 (March 1956) 10. Prose.
D142.   "All You Can Do Is Let It Rain." *The Grundtvig Review*,
         no. 5 (May 1956) 15. Poem.
D143.   "When We Were Here Together." *Liberation* I, 5 (July
         1956) 13. Poem.
D144.   "It's Because Your Heart is Pure, Honey." *The Needle* I,
         2 (July 1956) inside back cover. Poem.
         "Poemscapes: xvi, xvii, xviii, xxiii, xxv, xxvi, xxvii, xxviii,
         xxix, xxxvii, xl, xlii." *Poetry* LXXXIX (October 1956)
         31-42.
D146.   "The Origin of Baseball." *The Provincial* I, 1 (October
         1956) 3.

D147. "The Dog-Board." *Zero Anthlogy*, no. 8 (1956) 194. Poem. Includes a short note on Patchen.

D148. "Another Hamlet is Heard From." *Ark II, Moby I* (1956-1957) 34. Poem.

1957

D149. "The Only Thing That Was Full That Night Was the Moon," "Morning My Prince—the Eye That Walks," 'O What Do You See," "Just Outside Tombstone." *Miscellaneous Man*, no. 10 (January 1957) 1-2. Poems.

D150. "The Celery-Flute Player." *San Francisco Chronicle* (May 26, 1957) Drawing.

D151. "A Statement." *Coastlines* III, 1 (Winter, 1957-1958) 46. Prose statement, denying a connection with any regional poetry movement.

1958

D152. "Poemscapes XIX, XX, XXI, XXII," *New York Review* (Spring 1958) 27-28.

D153. "Two Christmas Poems: I have Lighted the candles, Mary; Nothing has changed," *Liberation*, III, 9 (December 1958) back cover.

1960

D154. "Had General Grant Been a Christmas Tree." *Liberation* V, 10 (December 1960) 16. Picture-poem.

1961

D155. "It Is Big Inside a Man." "Hand Me a Star." *Contact* II, 7 (February 1961) 1, 160. Poems; also a drawing by Patchen, 148. Issue is dedicated to Patchen.

D156. "Cabbage Croquettes," in "The Artists and Writers Cookbook." *Contact* II 7 (February 1961) 148. Recipe from Patchen's mother-in-law.

D157. "I'll Trade You Love for Glory," *Liberation* V, 12 (February 1961) 19. Picture-poem.

D158. "The Punch line: Pretty Soon Comes the Punch Line." *Liberation* VI, 1 (March 1961) 19. Picture-poem.

D159. "The Burso Dockle." *Liberation* VI, 3 (May 1961) 18-19. Picture-poem.

D160. "The Hunted City." *Metronome* LXXVIII, 8 (August 1961) 17. Poem.

D161. "The Lion Part." *Liberation* VI, 5 (Summer 1961) 25-26. Picture-poem.

D162. "Get Ready to Die." *Liberation* VI, 7 (September 1961) cover. Picture-poem.

D163. "Six Poems: When Was the Last Time You Saw an Uncolored Man?; I Got Me the Superstition Why Old Mr. Lousy's the No. One All the Time; Hark, Hark, Is It?; A Very Tall BeBop Pianist Trying to Dig the Scene at an Earwig-Watchers Convention; The Poor Little Guy; If There's One Thing I Don't Like It's a Two-Faced Headless Horseman." *Mendicant*, no. 1 (Autumn 1961) n.p. Poems and drawings.

D164. "Patchen page: When Was the Last Time You Saw an Uncolored Man?" "A Very Tall BeBop Pianist Trying to Dig the Scene at an Earwig-Watchers Convention," "Hark, Hark, Is It?" "I Got Me the Superstition Why Old Mr. Lousy's The No. One All the Time," "(What for You Be You So Bad All a Time?)." *Liberation* VI, 9 (November 1961) 19f. Picture-poems.

D165. "What is the beautiful?" "the murder of two men [from *Sleepers Awake*]," " 'it is the hour,' and '-and o my girl,' [both from *They Keep Riding Down All The Time*]." *the paper* I, 30 (December 31, 1961) n.p. First two are poems, other two prose.

D166. "Four Drawings." *Damascus Road*, no. 1 (1961) 41-44.

D167. "Oh 1$ For ALL RIGHT." *Journal For the Protection of ALL Beings* I, 1 (1961) 120. Picture-poem.

1962

D168. "Tribute to a Grandfather Foof." *Liberation* VI, 12 (February 1962) 23. Picture-poem.

D169. "O Take Heart My Brothers." *Liberation* VII, 1 (March 1962) 23. Picture-poem.

D170. "And So the Little Field Mouse Said," "My Program." *Liberation* VII, 3 (May 1962) 13-14. Picture-poems.

D171. "Eight Drawings." *Minnesota Review* II, 3 (Spring 1962) following page 304.

D172. "Let the World Be Any Man-Damned Way It Wants," "Can You Imagine What Would Happen," "Where Are the Other Rowboats?" "But I Wouldn't Be You," "Talk

like a Moose to Find an Angel in This Paradise," "If All
Goes Well (Or to Hell)," "Do You Suppose They're
Really as Bad as They Are?" *The Plumed Horn*, no. 3
(July 1962) 69-76. Picture poems, titles in Spanish on
76. Biographical notes on 125.

D173. "Paintings," *Outsider* I, 2 (Summer 1962) 84-88.

D174. "Peace or Perish." *Liberation* VII, 5 & 6 (Summer 1962)
20-21 (centerfold). Picture-poems.

D175. "At Three Five O'Clock," "There Is a Beautiful Place."
Vou [Japan], no. 86 (July-September 1962) 28. Picture-
poems.

D176. "Oh Come Now!" "Now, When I Get Back Here." *Liberation* VII, 8 (October 1962) 14-15. Picture-poems.

D177. "Defend Life!" *Coastlines*, no. 19 [V,3] (1962) inside back
cover. Poem.

1963

D178. "What Do You Say We Let It Shine." *Outsider* I, 3 (Spring
1963) 3. Picture-poem.

D179 "What Can You Do Up Here?" "The Best Hope." *Liberation* VII, 10 (December 1963) 14-15. Picture-poems.

D180 "Oh Come Now—There Is a Beautiful Place," "Peace
or Perish." *Eco Contemporaneo* [Spain], nos. 6/7 (1963)
112-113. Picture-poems.

1964

D181. "Whaleagle Rider," "Love, which includes Poetry,"
"Rode Him out of a Dream Maybe 10-12 Year Ago,"
"I'm with the Hunger Corpse," "The Easy Hat-Eye Went
to Sheperd's Krin," "All Is As It Is Not," "He's Either
Going Away or Coming Back," "Man Would You Just
Look at Your Leaders." — Eight Picture Poems. *Tri-
Quarterly* (Fall 1964) cover, and between pages 56
and 57.

D182. "The King of Toys," 'A Mercy-filled & defiant Xmas."
Motive XXV, 3 (December 1964) cover, 43. Painting-
poems.

D183. "Four Illustrated Manuscripts: O Take Heart my Brothers;
An Interview with the Floating Man; Sure Is One
Peculiar Way to Run a Ball Game; The Lion Part."
Notes From Underground I (1964) 13, 26, 27, 63. In-
cludes note on Patchen.

1965

D184.   "Glory and Love," "All Right, You May Alight." *Motive*
        XXV, 4 (January 1965) 23, inside back cover. Picture-
        poems.

D185.   "O Come Now!" "Now Is Then's Only Tomorrow," "Now
        When I Get Back Here." *The San Francisco Observer*
        I, 6 (April 26, 1965) back page. Picture-poems.

D186.   "All Right, You May Alight." *The San Fransicso Observer*
        I, 7 (May 3, 1975) Back page. Picture-poem.

D187.   "Berfu's Ox," "Snow Is the Only One of Us That Leaves
        No Tracks," "Is That All That's Wrong!" "The Scene
        of the Crime." *Stolen Paper Review*, no. 3 (Spring 1965)
        77-80. Picture-poems.

D188.   "What Are You Longing for, Shorty?" *Upriver: Currents
        of Poetry* I, 3 (Winter 1965) n.p. Picture-poems. Maga-
        zine dedicated to Patchen.

1966

D189.   "Two Picture-Poems: The Walking-Away World; Check!
        Questions Are the Best Things I Answer." *East-Side
        Review: A Magazine of Contemporary Culture* I, 1
        (January-February 1966) 52-53.

D190.   "If You Can Lose Your Head." *Motive* XXVII, 3 (Decem-
        ber 1966) back cover. Picture-poem.

1967

D191.   "Mika on Ihanaa?" *Sivu* [Finland] (March 10, 1967)
        5. Poem. Translation of "What Is the Beautiful?"

D192.   "The Way Men Live is a Lie," "What I'd Like To Know Is."
        Unicorn Folio I, 2 (April 15, 1967) n.p.

D193.   "If There's One Thing I Don't Like It's a Two-Faced
        Headless Horseman." *Mile-High Underground* I, 2
        (April 1967), cover. Poem. Reprinted from *Mendicant*.

D194.   "Sketches." *The Bay Guardian* I, 9 (May 19, 1967) 9.
        Drawings.

D195.   "Instructions for Angels," "Poemscapes II, X, XVII, XX,"
        "A Riddle for the First of the Month," "And with the
        Sorrows of this Joyousness," "I Am Timothy the Lion,"
        " 'Because He Kept Imagining a Pensive Rabbit,' " "For
        Miriam," "Elephants and Eskimos," "The Constant
        Bridegrooms," "What There Is," "A Parable at the

Year's End," "A Letter to God: Star," "But of Life."
Alameda County Weekender (September 16, 1967) 2-12.
Poems and picture-poems. Special issue on Patchen.

D196. "What Is the Beautiful?" *Naisten Vuri* [Finland] (November 10, 1967) 5.

D197. "Two Poems: I Have Lighted the Candles, Mary; When We Were Here Together." *Peace News* (December 22, 1967) 5.

1968

D198. "Come, Say Yes." *Joyful Noise*, no. 3 (May 1968) 2. Poem.

D199. "My God the Sorrow of It." *The Outsider* II, 4/5 (Winter 1968-1969), n.p. Picture-poem. Issue dedicated to Patchen.

D200. "O Take Heart, My Brothers," *Quaker Service*, no. 100 (Winter 1968-1969) 3. Picture-poem.

1969

D201. "Fra en Bly Pornografs Memoirer." *Selvysn: Aktuel Litteratur og Kulturdebat* [Norway] 10, 1 (September 1969) 8-14. Selection from *Memoirs of a Shy Pornographer*, with an introduction.

D202. "A Mercy Filled and Defiant Christmas to All Still Worthy to Be Called Men," "Lessons for the Feast of Christmas," "I Have Lighted the Candles, Mary," "Instructions for the Angels," "Wide, Wide in the Rose's Side," "No One Ever Works Alone." *Liturgy* XIV, 10 (December 1969) 1, 3, 8. Poems.

D203. "I Have Lighted the Candles, Mary." *Way* XXV, 10 (December 1969) 12. Poem.

D204. "Before the Bells of This New Year Ring." *Newsday/Viewpoint* (December 31, 1969) 1B. Poem.

1970

D205. "The Best Hope." *Association of California State College Professors* VI 6 (March 1970) 9. Picture-poem.

D206. "To Be Holy, Be Wholly Your Own." *The Massachusetts Daily Collegean* XCVIII, 134 (May 6, 1970) 6. Poem.

D207. "Peace For All Men or Amen To All Things." *AAUW Journal* LXIII, 4 (May 1970) 184. Picture-poem.

D208.   "Since we are not able." *Liturgy* XV, 7 (September 1970) cover. Poem.

D209.   "If Miracles Believed in Us." *Armadillo*, no. 2 (1970) cover. Picture-poem in full color.

1971

D210.   "An Easy Decision." *English Teaching Forum* IX 1 (January-February 1971) on recorded disc in magazine. Brief biographical sketch on 18.

D211.   "A Mercy-Filled and Defiant Xmas." *Mano-Mano* II, 10 (July 1971) 63-64. Poem in holograph. Magazine is dedicated to Patchen.

D212.   "Habitations," "Declaration of Peace." *The San Francisco Bay Guardian* (September 27, 1971) 25. Picture-poems.

D213.   "The Best Hope," "The One Who Comes to Question Himself," "And to Think It All Started out Like Any Other World," "Little Chief Son-of-a-Gun," "I Have a Funny Feeling," "The Issue Is No Longer War." *The Staff* (December 3, 1971) 32, 35, 37, 43. Picture-poems.

1972

D214.   "Crossing on Staten Island Ferry." *Los Angeles Free Press* (January 14, 1972) 23. Poem; also memorial note. Harry Redl photograph.

D215.   "O Take Heart, My Brothers." *The Sunday Paper* (February 17-23, 1972) 7A. Picture-poem.

D216.   "Words Getting People Crazier All the Time." *San Francisco Bay Guardian* (March 28, 1972) 11. Picture-poem.

D217.   "Rest, Heart of the Tired World." *Liturgy* XVII, 2 (March 1972) cover. Poem.

D218.   "What Was My World in All Truth." *Poetry* CXX, 1 (April 1972) inside back cover. Poem printed in memorium.

D219.   "What Is the Beautiful?" *New York Quarterly*, no. 9 (Winter 1972) 131. Memorial to the poet. Poem.

D220.   "Continuation of the Landscape." *Apple*, no. 7 (Autumn 1972) 1. Poem.

D221.   "Nice Staying, Hang in There, Friends." *The New York Quarterly*, no. 11 (Summer 1972) front cover. Picture-poem. Includes several drawings from *Hurrah for Anything* and two poems for Kenneth Patchen.

D222. "Klip af *The Journal of Albion Moonlight.*" *Dods Lay-outet* [Holland], no. 1 (1972) 7-19. Prose selection.

1973

D223. "Picture-Poem." *Peace News* (June 22, 1973) cover.

1974

D224. "Everyman Is Me," "We Deliver Us." *The Dakota Student,* (March 29, 1974) 9, 12. Picture-poems.

D225. "Poems of Sport: The Origin of Baseball." *Scholastic Voice* (April 18, 1974) 5. Poem.

1977

D226. "The Snow Is Deep On The Ground," "Poems Which Are Written By The Soul," "Wide, Wide In The Rose's Side," "Rest, Heart Of The Tired World." *Literary Cavalcade* XXIX, 6 (March 1977) 6-7. Poems.

D227. "Benediction for Mysterious Dolls." *The Black Cat*, no. 1 (1977) n.p. Poem.

E1.   THE CITY WEARS A SLOUCH HAT. One act. Written for the Columbia Radio Workshop (WBBM). Produced May 31, 1942. Music by John Cage.

E2.   DON'T LOOK NOW. Two acts. Productions:
  a. Troupe Theatre, Palo Alto, California, October 30, 1959.
  b. Thresholds, New York City, November 10, 1967. Produced as "Now You See It," per Patchen's wishes.
  c. Culver-Stockton College, Canton, Missouri, 1968.
  d. Kansas State University, Manhattan, Kansas, October 1970.

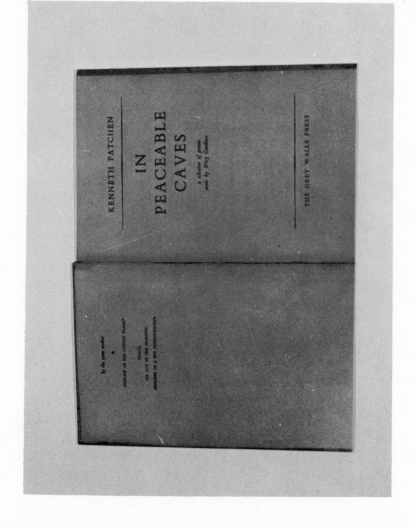

Title Page of *In Peacable Caves* (1950). A19.

Title Pages of *Fables and Other Little Tales* (1953). A21a.

F1.   KENNETH PATCHEN READS HIS POETRY WITH THE CHAMBER JAZZ SEXTET. Cadence CLP-3004, 1957.

F2.   KENNETH PATCHEN READS HIS SELECTED POEMS. Folkways 9717, 1959.
Contents: And What with the Blunders—The Origin of a Baseball—The Wolf of Winter—The Fox—Nice Day for a Lynching—23rd Street Runs into Heaven—Pastoral—The State of the Nation— 'Be Music, Night' —The Lions of Fire Shall Have Their Hunting—Red Wine and Yellow Hair—The Orange Bears—So Be It—The Everlasting Contenders—In Order To—The Man with the Golden Adam's Apple—Soon It Will—The Reason for Skylarks.

F3.   KENNETH PATCHEN READS WITH JAZZ IN CANADA (With the Alan Neil Quartet). Folkways 9718, 1959.
Contents: Four Blues Poems: (Comp. by Charlie Parker) —There's A Place—They Won't Let You In There—A Sigh is Little Altered—The Lonesome Boy Blues; Four Song Poems: (Comp. by George Wallington)—The Everlasting Contenders—Do I Not Deal With Angels—The Sea is Awash With Roses—Not Many Kingdoms Left; As I Opened The Window (Comp. by Dale Hillary)—Glory Glory (Arr. by Alan Neil)—Speeches from *Don't Look Now.*

F4.   KENNETH PATCHEN READS HIS LOVE POEMS. Folkways 9719, 1961.
Contents: Little Birds Sit on Your Shoulders—As Beautiful as the Hands of a Winter Tree—While the Sun Still Spends His Fabulous Money—O Now the Drenched Land Wakes—The Great Birds—Do I Not Deal with Angels—O She is as Lovely-Often—O My Darling Troubles Heaven—We Go Out Together—From My High Love—A Lament for the Unlasting Joys—Fall of the Evening Star—She Had Concealed Him—O My Love the Pretty Towns—Creation—The Character of Love Seen as a Search for the Lost—Religion is That I Love You—23rd Street Runs Into

Heaven—The Sea is Awash with Roses—As Frothing
Wounds of Roses—For Losing her Love—The Snow
is Deep on the Ground—As We Are so Wonderfully
Done with Each Other.

F5.   PATCHEN'S FUNNY FABLES. Green Tree Records
1972.
Contents: The evolution of the Hippopotamus—A Case
of Unmistakable Identity—Chicken Fried in Honey—
Gaunt Eva in the Mornin'—How the Slingshot Came to
Be Invented—The Professional Son—The Tale of
Rosie Bottom.

F6.   THE JOURNAL OF ALBION MOONLIGHT (Selections), Read by Kenneth Patchen. Folkways 9716, 1958.

SECTION G
MUSICAL AND FILM ADAPTATIONS

G1.   A DREAM OF THE SEVEN LOST STARS (1948). Music by David Bedford. Text taken from Patchen's "In Memory of Kathleen," from *First Will and Testament*. Universal (NYC).

G2.   BE MUSIC, NIGHT (1956). Music by David Diamond. Text is Patchen's poem of the same name. Carl Fischer (NYC).

G3.   MAIDEN SNOW (1961). Music by Richard Hundley. Text is Patchen's pooem of the same name. General Music Publishing Co. (NYC).

G4.   THE DARK KINGDOM (1966). Music by Richard Hensel. Words are a free adaptation of Patchen's book *The Dark Kingdom*. Associated Music Publishers (NYC).

G5.   GIVE YOU A LANTERN (1969). Music by Nelson Keyes. Text is Patchen's poem of the same name. Elkan-Vogel Co. (Philadelphia).

G6.   PLAGUE SUMMER (Date Uncertain). Animated Film by Chester Kessler. Based on *The Journal of Albion Moonlight*; scripted from same. Distributed by Audio Brandon (Mount Vernon, N.Y.).

G7.   WITH THIS ROSE I THEE WAKE (1975). Theatrical presentation setting much of Patchen's work to music. Ensemble Theatre Company (NYC). Done without authorization, resulting in a legal confrontation.

ABOUT PATCHEN

H 1.   Bishop, J.P. "Midnight of Sense." *Collected Essays*. New York: Scribners, 1948, pp. 295-296. General critical response to Patchen.

H 2.   Detro, Gene, ed. *Kenneth Patchen: The Last Interview*. Santa Barbara, California: Capra, 1976. Reprinted from *Outsider* 4/5 (1968) homage to Patchen (again reprinted in H10), with additional commentary by Miriam Patchen and Gene Detro.

H 3.   Dickey, James. "Kenneth Patchen." *Babel to Byzantium*. New York: Farrar, Straus & Giroux, 1968, pp. 71-72. General critical comment.

H 4.   Harte, Barbara, and Carolyn Riley, eds. "Kenneth Patchen." *200 Contemporary Authors*. Detroit: Gale Research Co., 1969, pp. 210-211. Biographical and bibliographical information.

H 5.   Hervey, Donald, ed. "Kenneth Patchen." *Recent American Literature*. Great Neck, New York: Burrows, 1958, p. 548. Biographical notes.

H 6.   Korte, Mary Norbert. "The Window: A Poem for the Death of Kenneth Patchen." *West to the Water - Six Poets; a Santa Cruz Portfolio*. Santa Cruz, California: The Lime Kiln Press, 1972, n.p.

H 7.   Kunitz, Stanley J. and Howard Haycraft, eds. "Kenneth Patchen." *Twentieth Century Authors*. New York: H.W. Wilson Co, 1942, pp. 1080-1081; repeated in first supplement, 1955. Primarily biographical information.

H 8.   Meltzer, David. *We All Have Something to Say to Each Other; being an essay entitled Patchen and four poems*. San Francisco: Auerhahn Press, 1962. Prose-poem essay bringing a personal and emotional focus to Patchen's life and work, followed by four poems by Meltzer.

H 9.   Miller, Henry. *Patchen, Man of Anger and Light*. New York: Max Padell, 1946. Literate essay on Patchen and his work, followed by an extended reaction to *The Journal of Albion Moonlight*. Reprinted in *Stand Still Like the Hummingbird*. NY: New Directions, 1962, and in H10.

H10.   Morgan, Richard G., ed. *Kenneth Patchen: A Collection of Essays*. New York: AMS Press, 1977. Includes most of the important critical and personal essays on Patchen, both published and unpublished, from 1936 to 1977, as well as selected reviews, a chronology, photographs, reproductions, and a selective bibliography. Introduction by Morgan, foreword by Miriam Patchen. See H2, H9, H13, H17, H18, J6, J13, J18, J32, J50, J65, J105, J119, J122, K36, K81, K138 and K166.

H11.   Murphy, Rosalie, ed. "Kenneth Patchen." *Contemporary Poets*. New York: St. Martin's Press, 1970, pp. 838-840. Biographical, critical, and bibliographical notes by David Meltzer.

H12.   Reuter, Laurel, ed. *Hallelujah Anyway!: a Kenneth Patchen Exhibition*. Grand Forks, North Dakota: University Art Gallery, 1974, 30 pp. Catalog of the exhibition of Patchen's picture-poems at the University of North Dakota March 18-April 5, 1974.

H13.   Rexroth, Kennth. "Kenneth Patchen, Naturalist of the Public Nightmare," *Bird in the Bush*. New York: New Directions, 1959, pp. 94-105. Primarily a response to *When We Were Here Together* and *Hurrah for Anything*, both published in 1957. Discusses Patchen's place in poetry and his methods, saying "Patchen is the only widely published poet of my generation who has not abandoned the international idiom of twentieth-century verse." Reprinted in H10.

H15.   Riley, Carolyn, ed. "Kenneth Patchen," *Contemporary Literary Criticism*. Detroit: Gale Research Co., 1973. p. 265. Biographical and critical notes.

H14.   Rexroth, Kenneth. "Kenneth Patchen," in James Vinson, ed. *Contemporary Novelists*. New York: St. Martin's Press, 1973. Biographical and bibliographical essay.

H16.   Warfel, Harry R. ed. "Kenneth Patchen," *American Novelists of Today*. New York: American Book Company, 1951, p. 337. Biographical sketch.

H17.   Wilder, A.N. "Revolutionary and Proletarian Poetry: Kenneth Patchen." *Spiritual Aspects of the New Poetry*. New York and London: Harper & Brothers, 1940, pp. 178-195. An expanded version of Wilder's essay in *Poetry*, LXI (April 1940). Reprinted in H10.

H18.   *Kenneth Patchen: Painter of Poems*. Baltimore: Gara-
         mond/Pridemark Press, 1969. Catalog of the exhibition
         of Patchen's picture-poems held December 12, 1969-
         January 18, 1970 at the Corcoran Gallery of Art in
         Washington, D.C. Accompanying material includes a
         biographical sketch by Miriam Patchen, an "apprecia-
         tion" by Richard Bowman (reprinted in H10), explana-
         tions of the procedures involved in the "painted books,"
         and a list of contributors to the exhibition.

H19.   *Tribute to Kenneth Patchen*. London: Enitharmon Press,
         1977. Personal "appreciations" of Patchen by William
         Everson, Lawrence Ferlinghetti, Howard Schoenfeld,
         Charles Wrey Gardner, James Schevill, Diane de Prima,
         Bernard Kops, Michael Horovitz, Joel Climenhaga,
         Hugo Manning, Lars Gustav Hellstrom, Jonathan
         Clark, and Diane Wald. Includes holography of "For
         Miriam (Since the tiny yellow rose)."

SECTION I
DISSERTATIONS

I1.   Nelson, Raymond J. *An American Mysticism: The Example of Kenneth Patchen.* DAI 30:5453A-54A. Stanford University, 1971. Patchen is examined as heir to the mystical tradition of America, particularly as related to Whitman.

I2.   Hogue, Herbert P. *The Anarchic Mystique of Five American Fictions.* DAI 32:1514A. University of Washington, 1972. One of the five is *The Journal of Albion Moonlight*, examined as a distintegration of self unified by the "voice" of the narrator.

I3.   Smith, Larry R. *The World of Kenneth Patchen: Form and Function in His Experimental Art.* DAI 35:6161A. Kent State University, 1974. Analysis of Patchen's work through a consideration of his personal aesthetics and beliefs.

I4.   Lozar, Tom. *An Introduction to Kenneth Patchen.* University of Toronto, 1977. Incisive examination of Patchen's background, and work by other poets of the period. A section is reprinted in H10.

J 1.   Anon. "Warren Youth Wins Guggenheim Award." *Warren* (Ohio) *Tribune-Chronicle* (April 1, 1936) 1. Patchen one of five poets to receive Guggenheim. His name is twice misspelled in the article.

J 2.   Anon. "Former Niles Man Now Rated as an Outstanding Poet." *Niles* (Ohio) *Times* (April 10, 1936) 1. Gives biographical background and records that *Before the Brave* was recently placed in the local library.

J 3.   Fitzgerald, R. "Footnotes to These Days." *Poetry* XLXII (September 1936) 340-342. Primarily a review of *Before the Brave*, though going beyond the book itself.

J 4.   Johnson, Roger C. "Young Poet Here to Seek Ideas." *Hollywood Citizen-News* (June 1, 1937) 3. Brief notice of Patchen's arrival in the area.

J 5.   Calmer, Alan. "Portrait of the Artist as a Proletarian." *Saturday Review of Literature* XVI, 14 (July 31, 1937) 3-4, 14. Discusses the Proletarian movement in literature, mentioning Patchen as an example.

J 6.   Wilder, A.N. "The Poet and the Class Struggle." *Poetry* LXI (April 1940) 32-39. Places Patchen's work in the political perspective of the times, particularly in relation to radical thought and Patchen's views on doctrine. Reprinted in H10 and H17.

J 7.   Untermeyer, Louis. "New Meanings in Recent American Poetry." *Virginia Quarterly Review* XVI, 3 (Summer 1940) 399-412. Discussion of Patchen on 408-409, commenting mainly on his technique in *First Will and Testament*.

J 8.   Anon. "Kenneth Patchen Writes New Book." *Warren* (Ohio) *Tribune-Chronicle* (August 27, 1940) 2. The book is *The Journal of Albion Moonlight*.

J 9.   Breit, Harvey. "Kenneth Patchen and the Critical Blind Alley." *Fantasy* VI, 4 (1940) 21-25. Discusses the reception of Patchen's first books and the difficulty of approaching him on traditional critical terms. Reprinted in H10.

J 10.   Anon. "Bookshop Notes." *Publishers Weekly* CXL (August 2, 1941) 320. Deals with the "launching" of

The Journal of Albion Moonlight at the Gotham Book Mart in New York City.

J 11. Weiss, T. "Kenneth Patchen and Chaos as Vision." *Briarcliff Quarterly* II (July 1946) 127-135. Highly negative essay, characterizing Patchen's writing as flabbiness and frenzy disguised as vision.

J 12. Fowler, Albert D. "The Man Who Writes Letters to God." *Fellowship* XII 10 (November 1946) 180-181. General critical essay concentrating on Patchen's humanism and hatred of war.

J 13. Gascoyne, David. "Introducing Kenneth Patchen." *Poetry Quarterly* VIII, 1 (Spring 1946) 4-10. Reprinted as the introduction to *Outlaw of the Lowest Planet* (1946), and in H10. Critical essay on Patchen's substance and method, relating him to Dada and other literary movements, and delineating his works to date.

J 14. Lyons, Richard. "A Note to Kenneth Patchen." *Circle* IX, (1946) 82. Poem criticizing Patchen.

J 15. Anon. "People in the Arts." *The Villager* (January 9, 1947) 6. Profile of Patchen.

J 16. Untermeyer, Jean Starr. "The Problem of Patchen." *Saturday Review of Literature* XXX (March 22, 1947) 15-16. General critical review of Patchen, centering on the works produced in 1946 and 1947.

J 17. Rogers, Howard Emerson. "A Note on Kenneth Patchen." *Occident* (Spring 1947) 29-33. Brief critical essay.

J 18. Taylor, Frajam. "Puck in the Gardens of the Sun." *Poetry* LXX (August 1947) 269-274. Examination of Patchen's poetry as reflected in *Selected Poems*. Reprinted in H10.

J 19. Eaton, Gail [Miriam Patchen]. "Kenneth Patchen: A First Bibliography." *Advance Guard* IV (1948) 107. Listing of Patchen's first six books.

J 20. Carlier, Marie. "Sketch of Kenneth Patchen." *Le Journal des Poetes* [France] V (June 1949) 1. Biographical notes.

J 21. Lesdain, Pierre. "Kenneth Patchen: Homme de Courroux et de Lumiere." *Le Journal des Poetes* V (June 1949) 4. Critical commentary.

J 22. Fletcher, Ian. "Stopping the Riot." *Nine* II (January 1950) 50-51. Critical comment on the intent of Patchen's work.

J 23. Heyer, Anselm. "Amerikanische Dichtung Nicht Ver-
deuscht." *Literaturblatt* [Denmark] (May 6, 1950)
6. Critical discussion of Emily Dickinson and Kenneth
Patchen.

J 24. Anon. *New York Times* (February 28, 1951) 25. "Six poets
to read [their works to raise funds for Patchen's medical
expenses.]" [The poets were W.H. Auden, E.E. Cummings, Archibald MacLeish, Marianne Moore, William
Carlos Williams and Edith Sitwell.]

J 25. Anon. "Benefit Reading for Kenneth Patchen." *Publishers Weekly* CLIX (March 10, 1951) 1269.

J 26. Anon. "Kenneth Patchen Fund." *Saturday Review of
Literature* XXXIV (March 31, 1951) 26.

J 27. Anon. *New York Times* (April 14, 1951) 13. Hofstra
students to give show to raise funds for Patchen's
operation.

J 28. Anon. "Poets Gather to Help a Poet." *Look* XXVII, 15
(June 19, 1951) 112. About the benefit reading for
Patchen.

J 29. Anon. "The Work of Kenneth Patchen." *Hartford Times*
(June 26, 1951) 2. Editorial praising Patchen and discussing his medical problems.

J 30. "Per Un Poeta Ammalato." *Tempo* [Italy] (June 1951) 24.
Concerns benefit for Patchen held to raise money for
treatment of his illness.

J 31. McGovern, Hugh. "Kenneth Patchen's Prose Works."
New Mexico Quarterly XXI (Summer 1951) 181-197.
Extensive examination of the major prose.

J 32. Glicksberg, Charles I. "The World of Kenneth Patchen."
Arizona Quarterly VII (Autumn 1951) 263-275. Discusses each of Patchen's works, in a perceptive and
favorable overview, picturing him as an apostle of
protest and faith, and reviewing criticism of his writing.
Reprinted in H10.

J 33. Ferling, Lawrence. "In the Hush of Concrete." *Counter-
point* XVII, 12 (December 1952) n.p. Ferling[hetti]
recalls a reading done with Patchen.

J 34. Anon. "Kenneth Patchen Wins Poetry Prize." *The Villager*
(December 31, 1953) 13. The prize was the Shelley
Memorial Award.

J 35. Anon. *New York Times* (November 20, 1955) 7. Comment
on Patchen's "painted books."

J 36. Gleason, Ralph J. "Patchen, Rexroth, and Box-Office Pull." *San Francisco Chronicle* (September 3, 1957) 22. Concerns Patchen and Rexroth's poetry-and-jazz readings.

J 37. Wilson, Russ. "Modern Poet, Jazz Combo Plan Debut." *Oakland Tribune* (October 3, 1957) 38. Preview of Patchen and the Chamber Jazz Sextet.

J 38. Nichols, Luther. "Poetry Mixes With Jazz." *San Francisco Examiner* (October 4, 1957). About Patchen at the Black Hawk in San Francisco.

J 39. Brown, Allen. "A Poet Tuned in to Night Club Jazz." *San Francisco Chronicle* (October 6, 1957) 14.

J 40. Stannard, Dick. "Jazzman in Rhymes." *Peninsula Living* (October 19-20, 1957) 10, 23. Concerns Patchen's poetry-and-jazz readings.

J 41. Gleason, Ralph J. "Perspectives." *Down Beat* XXIV (November 14, 1957) 20. Review and discussion of Patchen's first appearances at the Black Hawk in San Francisco, reading with the Chamber Jazz Sextet.

J 42. Anon. "Jazz Stars, Poet Land 'New' Theater." *Oakland Tribune* (November 18, 1957) 16E. Concerns plans for a jazz theatre for Patchen.

J 43. Anon. "Patchen Great in 'Dream Talk'." *Los Angeles Examiner* (December 30, 1957) 6. Concerns Patchen's readings with the Chamber Jazz Sextet.

J 44. McCarthy, Albert J. "Jazz and Poetry." *Jazz Monthly* (December 1957) 9-10. Discussion of the medium of poetry-and-jazz in general, and Patchen in particular.

J 45. Spencer, Elizabeth. "Niles-Born Poet, Kenneth Patchen, Is World Famous." *Niles* (Ohio) *Daily Times* (March 21, 1958) 1.

J 46. Michel, Don. "Marriage of Poetry and Jazz Performed by Patchen, Ferguson." *California Sun* (March 6, 1958) 2. Concerns Patchen's readings with the Chamber Jazz Sextet.

J 47. VonBlon, Katherine. "Concert Given by Jazz Men." *Los Angeles Times* (March 22, 1958) 3. Discusses concert by Patchen and the Chamber Jazz Sextet.

J 48. Reid, John T. "Contemporary Northamerican Lyric Poetry." *Estudios Americanos* XV (March-April, 1958) 145-155. Contains a short section on Patchen.

J 49.   May, James Boyer. "Towards Print." *Trace* XXVI (April 1958) 1-4. Includes a discussion of poetry-and-jazz, crediting Patchen with starting the movement.

J 50.   Yates, Peter. "Poetry and Jazz: III." *Arts and Architecture* (May 1958) 30-33. In-depth examination of Patchen's poetry-and-jazz combinations and of some of his other writing. Reprinted in H10.

J 51.   Dickey, James. "In the Presence of Anthologies." *Sewanee Review* LXVI, 2 (April-June 1958) 294-304. Section III concerns Patchen, analyzing his work as a compilation of notes, resulting in a frequently beautiful general vision.

J 52.   Anon. "P. A. Poet Kenneth Patchen to read work at world fair." *Daily Palo Alto Times* (July 8, 1958) 3. The fair was in Brussels, Belgium; Patchen was not ultimately able to go, due to illness.

J 53.   Nevins, Rex. "Meet Jazz Poet Patchen." *San Jose News* (July 17, 1958) 1. A profile.

J 54.   Smith, Cecil. "Poetry and Jazz on Video Menu." *Los Angeles Times* (August 25, 1958) 8. Previews Patchen's appearance on KABC's "Stars of Jazz" program.

J 55.   Ross, Annie. "The Blindfold Test." *Down Beat* XXV (September 4, 1958) 31. Concerns poetry and jazz readings by Patchen.

J 56.   Eckman, Frederick. "Comic Apocalypse of Kenneth Patchen." *Poetry* XCII (September 1958) 389-392. Review and discussion of several books; sees at once humor, rage, wonder and mysticism, likening Patchen to Blake. Reprinted in H10.

J 57.   Stainsby, Donald. " 'Jazz Poets' Rebel Against 'Stultifying Academic World.' " *The Vancouver Sun* (February 14, 1959) 5. General discussion of poetry-and-jazz, centering on Patchen.

J 58.   Anon. "Large Audience Digs Patchen's Poetry." *The Ubyssey* [Vancouver] (February 1, 1959) 1. Concerns Patchen reading at the University of British Columbia.

J 59.   Wilson, John S. "Jazz and Poetry Share Program." *New York Times* (March 17, 1959) 42. Notice of upcoming reading.

J 60.   Scleifer, Marc. "Kenneth Patchen on the 'Brat' Generation." *Village Voice* (March 18, 1959) 1, 7. Discusses

Patchen's poetry-and-jazz readings and his (generally negative) feelings about the San Francisco Beats.

J 61. Anon. "Patchen in Reading on Saturday." *San Francisco Examiner* (May 21, 1959) 4. Reading notice.

J 62. Farmer, Neita Crain. "Jazz wedded to poetry found exhiliarating." *Daily Palo Alto Times* (May 26, 1959) 19. Review of readings.

J 63. Anon. "Palo Alto poet-dramatist's first play opens tomorrow." *Daily Palo Alto Times* (October 29, 1959) 15. The play was *Don't Look Now* (E2). Patchen's first play was actually *The City Wears a Slouch Hat* (E1).

J 64. Anon. "Patchen play headed for off-Broadway." *Daily Palo Alto Times* (December 4, 1959) 16. *Don't Look Now* to be performed in New York.

J 65. Ciardi, John. "Kenneth Patchen: Poetry, and Poetry with Jazz." *Saturday Review of Literature* XLIII (May 14, 1960) 57. Considers experiments with poetry-and-jazz successful. Reprinted in H10.

J 66. Wilson, Keith C. "Kenneth Patchen; because he is." *Targets* 3 (September 1960) 24. An appreciation, discussing Patchen's medical problems.

J 67. Landau, Saul. "The Little World of the Holies." *Studies on the Left* I (Winter 1960) 84-88. Mention of Patchen and his relation to 'Other Beats' [sic].

J 68. Anon. "Appeal Voiced for Kenneth Patchen." *Oakland Tribune* (December 25, 1960) 19. Relates to Patchen's continuing medical problems.

J 69. Anon. "Tribute-benefits set for Kenneth Patchen." *Daily Palo Alto Times* (December 31, 1960) 5.

J 70. Anon. "Mingus Unit Heads Benefit Jazz Concert [for KP]." *Oakland Tribune* (January 1, 1961) B6.

J 71. Anon. "Patchen Tribute." *Daily Palo Alto Times* (January 4, 1961) 11.

J 72. Anon. "Musicians Play for Poet's Aid." *Oakland Tribune* (January 6, 1961) 23.

J 73. Anon. "Area library shows work of Patchen." *Daily Palo Alto Times* (January 11, 1961) 15. Exhibition of picture-poems at the Palo Alto Public Library.

J 74. Anon. "Two Tributes to Patchen Tomorrow." *Daily Palo Alto Times* (January 14, 1961) 9.

J 75. Anon. "SF backers plan tribute to Patchen." *Daily Palo Alto Times* (January 17, 1961) 9.

J 76. Anon. "Bay artists to auction work to aid Patchen." *Daily Palo Alto Times* (January 26, 1961) 13.

J 77. Anon. "Benefit Tomorrow for Poet Kenneth Patchen." *San Francisco Chronicle* (January 28, 1961) 17.

J 78. Anon. "An Artistic Tribute To an Ailing Poet." *San Francisco Examiner* (January 29, 1961) 3.

J 79. Rexroth, Kenneth. "Of Poets and Politics." *San Francisco Examiner* (January 29, 1961) 2. Discusses upcoming Patchen benefit.

J 80. Anon. "Patchen's Pals Put On Show." *San Francisco Examiner* (January 30, 1961) 28.

J 81. Anon. "Poet Patchen Returns Home from Hospital." *Daily Palo Alto Times* (January 31, 1961) 2.

J 82. See, Carolyn. "Kenneth Patchen: A Partial Bibliography." *Bulletin of Bibliography* XXIII (January-April 1961) 81-84. An incomplete checklist.

J 83. Anon. "Poet Patchen Recovering." *San Francisco News-Call Bulletin* (February 4, 1961) 2.

J 84. Wilcock, John. "Hurrah for Someone." *Village Voice* (February 16, 1961). Plea for help for Patchen.

J 85. Keown, Don. " 'Round Marin." *Independent Journal* (February 18, 1961) 16. On Patchen's illness and his latest contributions to *Contact* magazine.

J 86. Williams, Jonathan. "Out of Sight, Out of Conscience." *Contact* II (February 1961) 149-155. States that there is a "conspiracy of silence" concerning Patchen, discusses state of the artist in America, centering on Patchen. Reprinted in H10.

J 87. See, Carolyn. "The Jazz Musician as Patchen's Hero." *Arizona Quarterly* XVII (Summer 1961) 136-146. Relates experiments in jazz to the range of Patchen's work. Reprinted in H10.

J 88. Anon. Contributors' appeal, reprint from *Hurrah For Anything* ["It Is The Hour"]. *Venture* IV, 1 (1961) inside front cover.

J 89. Packard, William. "Letter to the Editor [on behalf of Kenneth Patchen]." *The Paper* I, 30 (December 31, 1961) n.p.

J 90. Hoppe, Art. "Nice Poem, Patchen, But It Don't Rhyme." *San Francisco Chronicle* (February 13, 1962) 37. Complimentary satirical article, proposing Patchen as American Poet Laureate.

J 91.   Thomas, Dante. "For Kenneth Patchen." *The Creative Review* II, 3 (Summer 1962) 1. Poem; other information on Patchen on the same page.

J 92.   Anon. "Poetry, Art, Books, Will be Highlights of Patchen Exhibit." *The Stanford Daily* (May 3, 1963) 1. Announces exhibit at Stanford, which ran through the month of May.

J 93.   Anon. "Poet Patchen spotlighted at Stanford." *Palo Alto Times* (May 9, 1963) 19. Relates to exhibit of silkscreens and painted books at the library and student union.

J 94.   Radcliffe, Charles and Diana Shelley. "Kenneth Patchen: Laureate of the doomed youth of the third world war." *Anarchy*, no. 34 (December 1963) 386-8. Discusses Patchen as a symbol of resistance and as a romantic.

J 95.   Rigg, Margaret. "Kenneth Patchen." *Motive* XXIV, 4/5 (January-February 1964) 53-61. 76. Concerns Patchen's life and work; also includes two drawings, three poems and nine picture-poems as follows: "I Have a Funny Feeling Because Growing a Mustache Was Pretty Tiring; Man Is Not a Town Where Things Live; The Dimensions of the Morning; Because My Hands Hear the Flowers Thinking; But What Can We Do?; Now Is Then's Only Tomorrow; My Program? The One Who Comes; Oh Come Now!; Elephants and Eskimos; Now When I Get Back Here."

J 96.   Dibble, Douglas. "The forgotten poet hero." *San Francisco Bay Guardian* I, 9 (May 19, 1967) 1. A personal view of Patchen.

J 97.   Nelson, Raymond. "Is Patchen Ready for the Academy." *The San Francisco Bay Guardian* I, 9 (May 19, 1967) 9. Critical perspective, concluding that though Patchen is not banal enough for academe, room should nevertheless be made for him.

J 98.   Anon. *New York Times* (July 6, 1967) 40. National Endowment for the Arts makes its awards, including one to Patchen.

J 99.   Vendler, Helen. "Recent American Poetry." *Massachusetts Review* VIII (Summer 1967) 641-660. Includes a brief section on Patchen.

J100.   Anon. "A Bay Area Poet's Fight Against Pain." *Alameda County Weekender* (September 16, 1967). Special twelve-page supplement on Patchen. Includes brief interview by Douglas Dibble, notes by Gene Detro and Ray Nelson, and work by Patchen reprinted from *Poemscapes* (1958), *Because It Is* (1960), *Hurrah for Anything* (1957), and "A Letter to God" from *Doubleheader* (1965).

J101.   Celly, Jean-Jacques. "English Language Poetry: Le Theme de l' Amour chez W.B. Yeats, D.H. Lawrence, et Kenneth Patchen." *Poesie Vivante* [France], nos. 25/26 (November 1967) 103-105. Comparative article: poems printed in French and in English.

J102.   Anon. "Patchen Great in 'Dream Talk'." *Los Angeles Examiner* (December 30, 1967) 6. Comment on *Don't Look Now*.

J103.   Glover, David. "The Horror and the Hope." *Avatar* (March 1-13, 1968) 5-7. Extended critical and biographical article centering on the picture-poems, but including other works as well. Reprinted in *Kaleidoscope* (J104).

J104.   Glover, David. "The Horror and the Hope." *Kaleidoscope* I, 15 (May 24-June 6, 1968) 2, 10-12. Reprinted from *Avatar* (J103).

J105.   Webb, Jon and Louise, eds. *The Outsider*, nos. 4/5 (1968). Special issue: "Homage to Kenneth Patchen." Contains notes, appreciations and brief essays on Patchen by Norman Thomas, Brother Antoninus, Allen Ginsberg, James Boyer May, Harold Norse, Millen Brand, Hugh MacDiarmid, David "Tony" Glover, Kenneth Rexroth, John William Corrington, Bern Porter, Lawrence Ferlinghetti, David Meltzer, Lafe Young, Jack Conroy, Frederick Eckman, Henry Miller (from H9; reprinted in H10), an interview by Gene Detro (reprinted in H10 and H19), a holograph reproduction of a letter from Miriam Patchen, and a selection of photographs of Patchen from various sources.

J106.   Nelson, Ray. "The Moral Prose of Kenneth Patchen." *Steppenwolf* III (Summer 1969) 59-86. A thorough academic essay on the prose works and their relation to literary and historical movements. Reprinted in H10.

J107.   Margolis, Barba, "Patchen." *The Staff* (December 3, 1971) Part two, 35, 37. Personalized critical and biographical essay on Patchen, concerned in large part with the picture-poems.

J108. Anon. *San Francisco Examiner and Chronicle* (January 9, 1972) 8. Obituary.

J109. Anon. "City Loses Famed Son In Death of Patchen." *Warren* (Ohio) *Tribune-Chronicle* (January 11, 1972) 5. Obituary.

J110. McReynolds, David. "You're a bastard mr. death." *The Sunday Paper* (February 17-23, 1972) 7A. Memorial article. Reprinted in the *L.A. Free Press* (J128).

J111. Ferlinghetti, Lawrence. "An Elegy on the Death of Kenneth Patchen." *San Francisco Sunday Examiner and Chronicle: This World* (March 5, 1972) 33. Poem.

J112. Ritter, Jess. "Minstrel's Memorial: Shreds of Patchen." *Village Voice* (March 9, 1972) 21. Discusses a Memorial Reading for Patchen.

J113. Margolis, Susan. "Paying Homage to Kenneth Patchen." *California Living* (March 12, 1972) 40-5.

J114. Margolis, Susan. "A Reading for Kenneth Patchen." *Rolling Stone* (March 16, 1972) 26. Concerns the Memorial Tribute to Patchen in San Francisco.

J115. McReynolds, David. "You Bastard, Mr. Death." *Los Angeles Free Press: Arts Supplement* (March 17, 1972) 2. Reprinted from *The Sunday Paper* (J123).

J116. Kamstra, Jerry. "Some Last Thoughts on Kenneth Patchen." *The San Francisco Bay Guardian* (March 28, 1972) 11. Memorial article.

J117. Hammond, Henry. "Kenneth Patchen: Literary and Graphic Artist." *Gob, A Poetry Magazine* I, 2-3 (April 1972) 15-17. General critical essay; also a review of *Wonderings*.

J118. Tibbs, Ben. "Remembering Kenneth Patchen 1911-1972." *Westigan Review of Poetry* II, 3(1972) 30. An appreciation.

J119. Hack, Richard. "Memorial Reading for Kenneth Patchen at City Lights Poets Theatre San Francisco: February 2, 1972." *Chicago Review* XXIV, 2 (1972) 65-80. An extensive description of the reading, followed by an impressionistic discussion of the *Journal of Albion Moonlight*. Reprinted in H10.

J120. Frankenstein, Aflred. "Patchen's Search for a 'Beautiful World'." *San Francisco Examiner & Chronicle* (January 28, 1973) 38. An appreciation.

J121.   Anon. "Patchen exhibit in gallery 'visual poem'." *The Dakota Student* LXXXVIII, 45 (March 20, 1974). Concerns the exhibit of painting-poems in the University of North Dakota Art Gallery, March 18-April 5, 1974.

J122.   Shevill, James. "Kenneth Patchen: The Search for Wonder and Joy." *American Poetry Review* V, 1 (January-February 1976) 32-6. Extensive, perceptive critical and biographical examination of Patchen and his work. Reprinted in H10.

Note: Some of the reviews cited were brought to my knowledge through scrapbooks the Patchens kept from 1934 to 1963, which are now housed at the University of California at Santa Cruz. As the items exist there only as clippings, many do not have page numbers or complete date or publication information. In many cases, I have been able to supply the missing information. Where files of the newspaper or periodical were not available to me and the entry is therefore incomplete, I have indicated that it is from the scrapbooks by placing an asterisk (*) after the entry.

Before the Brave

K 1. Wagner, Charles A. "Books." *New York Daily Mirror* (January 27, 1936)*

K 2. Hansen, Harry. "The First Reader." *New York World-Telegram* (February 5, 1936)*

K 3. *Syracuse* (NY) *Herald* (February 5, 1936)*

K 4. *Providence* (RI) *News-Tribune* (February 6, 1936)*

K 5. Lewis, Jay. "Books and Authors." *Norfolk* (VA) *Ledger Dispatch* (February 7, 1936)*

K 6. *Houston* (TX) *Press* (February 8, 1936)*

K 7. *San Mateo* (CA) *Times* (February 8, 1936) 6.

K 8. *Ashland* (KY) *Independent* (February 9, 1936)*

K 9. Ellingson, H.K. *Colorado Springs Gazette* (February 9, 1936)*

K 10. Fraser, Abbott. "Two Poets Look at the Future, Philosophically." *Charlotte* (NC) *News* (February 9, 1936)*

K 11. Long, Hamiel. *Time* XXVII, 6 (February 10, 1936) 74-75.

K 12. *San Francisco News* (February 11, 1936)*

K 13. *Norfolk* (VA) *Pilot* (February 12, 1936)*

K 14. *Wyandotte* (MI) *News* (February 14, 1936)*

K 15. *Cleveland* (OH) *News* (February 15, 1936)*

K 16. Benet, W.R. "Phoenix Nest." *Saturday Review of Literature* XIII, 16 (February 15, 1936) 26.

K 17. *Macon* (GA) *Telegraph & News* (February 16, 1936)*

K 18. Seaver, Edwin. "Books and Authors." *Sunday Worker* (February 16, 1936)*

K 19. *Middletown* (CT) *Press* (February 18, 1936)*

GLORY NEVER GUESSES

to Miriam

Being a collection of 18 poems
with decorations and drawings
reproduced through silk screening
from the original MS. pages of
Kenneth Patchen

The Animal That Walks Sitting Down • Who Are You • In The Patient Eye • From "The Tea-Kettle Suggestion" • Keep It • Counsel For The Offense • The Monument-Maker • An Old Lady Named Amber Sam • The Sun-Man King Of Logoona • Glory Never Guesses • If You Can Lose Your Head • The Smallest Giant In The World • To "Run The Crown" House On Horseback • The Moment The Peacock • Garrity The Gambling Man

SILK SCREEN REPRODUCTION BY FRANK BACHER
IN A HAND-RUN EDITION OF 200 COPIES
ON HANDMADE JAPANESE PAPERS

10ᵃᵃ

Cover of *Glory Never Guesses* (1955). A24.

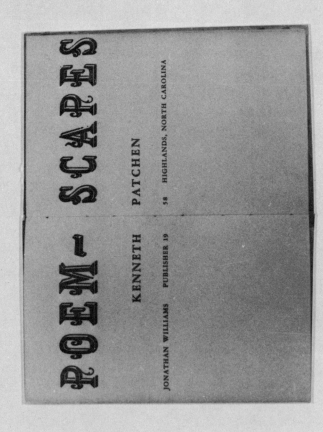

Title Pages of *Poemscapes* (1958). A28d.

K 20.   Issacs, Norman E. "Times Books." *Indianapolis Times* (February 20, 1936)*

K 21.   Avrett, Robert. "Radical in Rhymes." *El Paso* (TX) *Herald Post* (February 21, 1936)*

K 22.   *Desert News* (Salt Lake City, UT) (February 22, 1936)*

K 23.   *Sacramento* (CA) *Bee* (February 22, 1936)*

K 24.   *Omaha* (NE) *World-Herald* (February 23, 1936)*

K 25.   "Poet of Proletariat." *The Delmarva* (DE) *Star* (February 23, 1936)*

K 26.   *Birmingham* (AL) *News* (February 23, 1936)*

K 27.   *Portland Oregonian* (February 23, 1936)*

K 28.   Ford, Sidney Holland. "Poet's Travels Are Reflected." *Houston* (TX) *Post* (February 23, 1936)*

K 29.   Lowe, Howard. "Versification of Class War." *San Francisco Chronicle* (February 23, 1936) 5D.

K 30.   *Springfield* (MA) *Union* (February 24, 1936)*

K 31.   *Baltimore* (MD) *Evening Sun* (February 29, 1936)*

K 32.   Fearing, Kenneth. *Book Union Bulletin* (February 1936)*

K 33.   *High Point* (NC) *Enterprise* (March 1, 1936)*

K 34.   Shaw, Tom, Jr. "Book Slants." *Greensboro* (NC) *Record* (March 2, 1936)*

K 35.   *Southbridge* (MA) *News* (March 13, 1936)*

K 36.   Deutsch, Babette. "A Poet of the Steel Works." *New York Herald Tribune Books* (March 15, 1936) 7. Reprinted in H10.

K 37.   Lanman, C. Richard. "Contrast in Style." *Atlanta* (GA) *Constitution* (March 15, 1936) 3k.

K 38.   *Los Angeles Times* (March 15, 1936)*

K 39.   *Dayton* (OH) *News* (March 20, 1936)*

K 40.   *San Diego* (CA) *Union* (March 22, 1936)*

K 41.   Preece, Harold. "Youth Speaks in Poetry." *World Youth* (March 28, 1936) 4.

K 42.   *Booklist* XXXII (March 1936) 196.

K 43.   Rosenberg, Harold. *Partisan Review* III, 2 (March 1936) 30.

K 44.   Rodman, Selden. *Common Sense* (March 1936)*

K 45.   McCreary, William Harold. "Left Wing Poetry." *Louisville* (KY) *Herald-Post* (April 5, 1936)*

K 46.   *Springfield* (MA) *Republican* (April 7, 1936) 10.

K 47.   *Christian Century* LIII, 15 (April 8, 1936) 539.

K 48.   Stone, Geoffrey. *American Review* VII (April 1936) 103.

K 49.   Long, Haniel. *Survey Graphic* XXV (April 1936) 256.

K 50.   *San Francisco News* (May 2, 1936)*
K 51.   Kaufman, Samuel A. "Today's New Books." *Brooklyn*
        (NY) *Times-Union* (May 12, 1936)*
K 52.   Quinn, Kerker. *New Republic* LXXVII, 1123 (June 10,
        1936) 138-139.
K 53.   Walton, Eda Lou. "Three Young Marxist Poets." *New*
        York Times Book Review (June 21, 1936) 16.
K 54.   Leach, H.G. *Forum* LXXXVI (August 1936) 96.

First Will and Testament

K 55.   Bryant, Helen. "Wills and Testaments." *Poetry World*
        XI, 2-5 (September-December 1939) 52-56.
K 56.   Thompson, Norman. *Hollywood* (CA) *Citizen-News*
        (November 11, 1939)*
K 57.   *New Yorker* XV, 40 (November 18, 1939) 108.
K 58.   Benet, W.R. "Phoenix Nest." *Saturday Review of Liter-*
        ature XXI, 5 (November 25, 1939) 16.
K 59.   *Greensboro* (NC) *News* (November 26, 1939)*
K 60.   Bishop, J.P. *Nation* CXLIX, 22 (December 2, 1939)
        620-621.
K 61.   *The Providence Journal* (December 17, 1939) Sec. VI, 6.
K 62.   Goldgar, Harry. "Today's Book." *The Macon* (GA) *Tele-*
        graph (December 19, 1939)*
K 63.   Lechlitner, Ruth. "Poems for This Age of Shadows."
        New York Herald Tribune Books (December 24, 1939) 5.
K 64.   Mowrer, Deane. "The Waste Land: 1939." *New Republic*
        CI, 1308 (December 27, 1939) 294.
K 65.   *Cincinnati* (OH) *Enquirer* (December 30, 1939) 5.
K 66.   Walton, Eda Lou. "Kenneth Patchen's Poems." *New York*
        Times Book Review (January 21, 1940) 17.
K 67.   *Common Sense* (January 1940) 26.
K 68.   Fuller Roy. "Recent Verse." *The New English Weekly*
        (February 29, 1940) 282-283.
K 69.   *Living Age* CCCLVII (February 1940) 579.
K 70.   Wheelwright, John. *Compass* II, 2/3 (February 1940)
        59-61.
K 71.   Aiken, Conrad. "Poetry: 1940 Model." *New Republic*
        CII, 17 (April 22, 1940) 540-541.
K 72.   Maynard, Theodore. "The New Artificiality." *Virginia*
        Quarterly Review XVI, 2 (Spring 1940) 311-315.
K 73.   Rosenfeld, Paul. "On Reading Patchen's New Poems."
        The University Review VI, 4 (June 1940) 282-283.

K 74. Millspaugh, C.A. "Among the New Books of Verse." *Kenyon Review* II, 3 (Summer 1940) 359-363.

K 75. Brown, Ray C.B. "Dust Bins and Stars." *Voices* C (Winter 1940) 46-49.

The Journal of Albion Moonlight

K 76. Miller, Henry. *Experimental Review*, no. 2 (November 1940) 72-73.

K 77. Rosenfeld, Paul. "The Life of the Hunted." *The Nation* CLIII, 13 (September 27, 1941) 286-288.

K 78. Whittemore, Reed, Jr. "Surrealism in Wartime." *New York Herald-Tribune Books* (October 12, 1941) 14.

K 79. Mattick, Paul. "To Be or Not to Be." *Decision* III, 1-2 (January-February 1942) 80-82.

K 80. Fitts, Dudley. "Experiments in Life and Death." *Accent* II, 2 (Winter 1942) 112-115.

K 81. Williams, William Carlos. "A Counsel of Madness." *Fantasy* X, 2 (1942) 102-107. Reprinted in H10.

K 82. Lowell, Jean Stafford. "Walpurgis Nacht, 1940." *Kenyon Review* IV (1942) 106-108.

K 83. Kirsch, Robert R. "A Kind of Sense Out of Madness." *The Book Report* (September 19, 1961)*

The Dark Kingdom

K 84. Scott, W.T. *Providence* (RI) *Sunday Journal* (March 22, 1942) 6.

K 85. Jack, Peter M. "The New Books of Poetry." *New York Times Book Review* (March 29, 1942) 4.

K 86. Dransfield, Jane. "The Book of the Day." *New York Sun* (April 29, 1942)*

K 87. Benet, W.R. *Saturday Review of Literature* XXV, 19 (May 9, 1942) 14.

K 88. Breit, Harvey. "On a Bronze Horse." *Poetry* LX (June 1942) 160-163.

K 89. Warren, Robert Penn. "Poems by Kenneth Patchen." *Nation* CLV, 1 (July 4, 1942) 17.

K 90. Alling, Kenneth Slade. "Two Poets and Two Kingdoms." *Voices*, no. 110 (Summer 1942) 46-48.

K 91. Quinn, Kerker. "Some Other Way in Verse." *New York Herald Tribune Books* (September 13, 1942) 14.

K 92. *Crescendo* II, 1 (Autumn 1942) 18.

K 93. Duncan, Robert. *Accent* II, 1 (Autumn 1942) 64.

The Teeth of the Lion

K 94.   Deutsch, Babette. "Poets Timely and Timeless." *New Republic* CVIII, 1478 (March 29, 1943) 420.

K 95.   Honig, Edwin. *Poetry* LXII (August 1943) 284.

K 96.   Drew, Elizabeth. *New York Herald-Tribune Books* (September 19, 1943) 23.

K 97.   Comfort, Alex. *Poetry Quarterly* V, 4 (Winter 1943) 149-151.

K 98.   Untermeyer, Louis. *Yale Review* XXXIII (Winter 1944) 351.

Cloth of the Tempest

K 99.   *The Providence* (RI) *Journal* (October 10, 1943) Sec. IV, 8.

K 100. Benet, W.R. *Saturday Review of Literature* XXVI, 42 (October 16, 1943) 64.

K 101. Foff, Arthur. "Poet of Varied Moods." *San Francisco Chronicle* (October 17, 1943) 14.

K 102. Weiss, T. *Quarterly Review of Literature* I, 1 (Autumn 1943) 59-66.

K 103. Schiff, Sarah. *Springfield* (MA) *Republican* (November 5, 1943) 10.

K 104. *Los Angeles Times* (November 7, 1943)*

K 105. Kennedy, Leo. *Chicago Sun Book Week* (November 7, 1943) 7.

K 106. Davis, R.G. *New York Times Book Review* (November 21, 1943) 42.

K 107. Poster, William. "Some Recent Verse." *New Republic* CIX, 25 (December 20, 1943) 890.

K 108. *Living Poetry* (Winter 1943)*

K 109. Rittenhouse, Jessie B. "Youth is Experimental." *Palisade* (Winter 1943) 86-87.

K 110. *The Sonneteer* I (Winter 1943-1944) 15.

K 111. Lazarus, H.P. "Poetry in Review." *Nation* CLVIII, 3 (January 15, 1944) 80.

K 112. Manners, David X. "Pacifist Poets." *Conscientious Objector* (January 1944) 5.

K 113. Bogan, Louise. *New Yorker* XX (February 26, 1944) 82.

K 114. Forgotson, E.S. "Patchen's Progress." *Poetry* LXII (February 1944) 278-280.

K 115. Shapiro, Leo. "Patchen's Cloth, Gregory's Triumph." *Voices*, no. 123 (Winter 1944) 51-53.

Memoirs of a Shy Pornographer

K116. Carmer, Carl. "An Artesian Well of words and ideas." P.M. (September 15, 1945) 13-14.

K117. Trilling, Diana. "Fiction in Review." *Nation* CLXI, 12 (September 22, 1945) 292.

K118. Bender, R.J. "Buffoonery, Wit, and Very Free Association." *Chicago Sun Book Week* (September 23, 1945) 15.

K119. Winebaum, B.V. *New York Times Book Review* (October 7, 1945) 32.

K120. Randolph, John. "A Queer Lot of Characters Flit Through Odd Novel." *Chicago Tribune* (October 7, 1945).

K121. *New Yorker* XXI (October 27, 1945) 94.

K122. Webster, Harvey Curtis. "Pornographic Surrealism." *Louisvile* (KY) *Courier-Journal* (October 28, 1945) 12.

K123. Rosenfield, Isaac. "Avante-Garde Comedy." *New Republic* CXIII, 23 (December 3, 1945) 772-774.

K124. Ingallis, Jeremy. *Saturday Review of Literature* XXVIII, 51 (December 22, 1945) 26.

K125. Gee, Kenneth. "The Adventures of Albert Budd." *The New English Weekly* XXIII (February 14, 1946) 175.

K126. *The Miami* (FL) *Herald* (July 7, 1946)*

K127. Finch, Roy. "Prophetic Dreams." *The Conscientious Objector* (1946)*

An Astonished Eye Looks Out of the Air

K128. Stanford, Derek. *Poetry Quarterly* VIII, 3 (Autumn 1946) 182-184.

Outlaw of the Lowest Planet

K129. Lewis, N. "Two Worlds." *The Times* [London] *Literary Supplement* 2330 (September 28, 1946) 467.

K130. Dern, Paul. *Time and Tide*, XXVII, 44 (November 2, 1946) 1054.

K131. Owen, G.E.L. "American Poet." *The Isis* XXXVIII (November 6, 1946) 23.

K132. "Poetry Running to Waste." *Truth* (November 8, 1946)*

Selected Poems

K133. *Chicago Tribune* (December 22, 1946)*
K134. Berryman, John. "Lowell, Thomas, & c." *Partisan Review* XIV, 1 (January-February 1947) 73-85, p. 83 on Patchen.
K135. Schwartz, Delmore. "I Feel Drunk All the Time." *Nation* CLXIV, 8 (February 22, 1947) 220.
K136. Untermeyer, Louis. *Saturday Review of Literature* XXX, 12 (March 22, 1947) 16.
K137. Avison, Margaret. *Canadian Forum* XXVII (April 1947) 21.
K138. Taylor, Frajam. *Poetry* LXX (August 1947) 269. Reprinted in H10.
K139. Swallow, Alan. *New Mexico Quarterly* XVIII, 4 (1948) 45.

Sleeper Awake

K140. *Chicago Tribune* (June 30, 1946)*
K141. Basso, Hamilton, *New Yorker* XXII (July 6, 1946) 57.
K142. Shepherd, Marshall. "Man and his World." *The Nashville* (TN) *Banner* (October 9, 1946) 18.

Pictures of Life and of Death

K143. Risen, William. *Cincinnati* (OH) *Enquirer* (September 25, 1947)*

See You In The Morning

K144. *Norfolk* (VA) *Ledger-Dispatch* (January 14, 1948)*
K145. *Manchester* (NH) *Union-Leader* (January 1948)*
K146. *The* (Charleston, SC) *News and Courier* (February 8, 1948)*
K147. *Hartford* (CT) *Courant Magazine* (February 29, 1948)*
K148. *The San Diego* (CA) *Union* (February 29, 1948)*
K149. *Daily Oklahoman* (March 7, 1948)*
K150. *Montgomery* (AL) *Advertiser* (March 21, 1948)*
K151. *The Providence* (RI) *Journal* (March 21, 1948) Sec. VI, 8.
K152. Neal, S.M. *Springfield Republican* (March 21, 1948) 12B.
K153. *San Francisco Chronicle* (March 21, 1948) 21.
K154. *Burlington* (VT) *Free Press* (March 27, 1948)*
K155. *Emporia* (KS) *Gazette* (April 9, 1948)*
K156. Balakian, Nona. *New York Times Book Review* (April 18, 1948) 16.
K157. *Chicago Tribune* (April 25, 1948)*

Red Wine and Yellow Hair

K158.   *Kirkus* XVII (February 1, 1949) 82.

K159.   Nims, John Frederick. "Lively Verse Holds Its Basic Theme." *Chicago Sunday Tribune* (February 13, 1949) Part IV, 1.

K160.   Saul, George Brandon. "Significant Sound and Fury." *Hartford* (CT) *Courant* (February 13, 1949)*

K161.   McDonald, Gerald. *Library Journal* LXXIV (March 15, 1949) 497.

K162.   McDonald, Gerald. *Nation* CLXVII, 14 (April 2, 1948) 396.

K163.   Fitts, Dudley. *Saturday Review of Literature* XXXII, 29 (July 16, 1949) 37.

K164.   Lechlitner, Ruth. *New York Herald-Tribune Books* (July 31, 1949) 4.

K165.   Davidson, Eugene. *Yale Review* XXXVIII (Summer 1949) 725.

K166.   Hall, James. *Poetry* LXXV (November 1949) 75. Reprinted in H10.

K167.   Lowe, Robert. *Furioso* V, 1 (1950) 72.

Fables and Other Little Tales

K168.   Ferling, Lawrence. "Reviews of Some of the New Books of Poetry." *San Francisco Chronicle* (June 13, 1954) 18, 21.

The Famous Boating Party

K169.   Rodman, Selden. "More Fun Than Winning." *New York Times Book Review* (August 1, 1954) 4, 15.

Poems of Humor and Protest and
A Surprise for the Bagpipe Player

K170.   "Poetry in the 'soft shell' fills a niche." *San Francisco Chronicle* (September 23, 1956) 27.

Selected Poems, Enlarged Edition

K171.   Maslin, Marsh. "The Browser." *San Francisco Call-Bulletin* (February 13, 1958) 9.

K172.   Justice, Donald. *Western Review* XXII (Spring 1958) 231-234.

K 173.   Eberhart, Richard. "Central Violence." *Saturday Review of Literature* XLI, 28 (July 12, 1958) 30-32.

K 174.   Eckman, Frederick. *Poetry* XCII (September 1958) 389.

K 175.   Benedict, Michael. "Choices and Risks." *Poetry* CV (February 1965) 332-334.

K 176.   Sorrentino, Gilbert. "Pariahs on Parnassus." *Chicago Sun Book Week* (August 8, 1965)*

Hurrah For Anything

K 177.   *Trace* no. 22 (June 1957) 23.

K 178.   Pope, R.L. *Poetry Broadside* I, 3 (Winter, 1957-1958) 9.

K 179.   Holmes, John. "A Wild World of His Own." *New York Times Book Review* (February 2, 1958) 5.

K 180.   Baum, Robert. *Poetry* II (September 1958) 384.

When We Were Here Together

K 181.   Stanford, Ann. "World is Good, Though Spoiled by Man, Poet Patchen Believes." *Los Angeles Times* (December 8, 1957) Part V, 9.

K 182.   Holmes, John. "A Wild World of His Own." *New York Times Book Review* (February 2, 1958) 5.

K 183.   Flatto, Elie. *Village Voice* (February 12, 1958) 9.

K 184.   McDonald, Gerald. *Library Journal* LXXXIII (April 1, 1958) 1099.

K 185.   Wright, James. *Yale Review* XLVII (June 1958) 610.

K 186.   Eckman, Frederick. *Poetry* XCII (September 1958) 390.

Poemscapes

K 187.   Eberhart, Richard. *New York Times Book Review* (June 22, 1958) 4.

K 188.   Ciardi, John. *Saturday Review of Literature* XLI, 39 (September 27, 1958) 19.

K 189.   Eckman, Frederick. *Poetry* XCII (September 1958) 391.

Don't Look Now (Now You See It.)

K 190.   "A Poet's Play Bubbles in Theatre's Test Tube." *Peninsla Living* (October 24-25, 1959) 11, 13.

K 191.   Hamilton, Francis. "Patchen Play Is For Inner Ear." *San Francisco News-Call Bulletin* (October 31, 1959) 7.

K192. Nichols, Dorothy. "Don't Look Now: Patchen's first play shown in Palo Alto." *Daily Palo Alto* (CA) *Times* (October 31, 1959) 9.

K193. "Play-goers see two premieres in Palo Alto." *Daily Palo Alto* (CA) *Times* (October 31, 1959) 4.

K194. "Patchen Play is New Treatment of Old Idea." *San Mateo* (CA) *Times* (November 3, 1959) 3.

K195. Janss, Betty. "Patchen Play a Fantasy." *San Francisco Chronicle* (November 3, 1959) 36.

K196. *Daily Palo Alto* (CA) *Times* (November 27, 1959) 13.

K197. *New York Times* (November 20, 1967), Section Two, 1.

Kenneth Patchen Reads With Jazz In Canada

K198. Dalva, Edward. "The Duke." *San Mateo* (CA) *Times* (November 7, 1959)*

K199. "A Potent Draught of Poetry-With-Jazz." *Oakland* (CA) *Tribune* (November 15, 1959) 23B.

Recording: Kenneth Patchen Reads His Poetry With The Chamber Jazz Sextet

K200. *Downbeat* XXVI (May 14, 1959) 25.

Selected Poems Read By Kenneth Patchen

K201. Hough, Henry W. "Readings Put to Jazz." *San Francisco Chronicle* (April 27, 1958) 12.

The Love Poems

K202. Fuller, John. "Protest and Gruel." *Time and Tide* XLII (February 17, 1961) 256.

K203. Bell, Marvin. "Thoughts Upon a New Kenneth Patchen Book." *Trace*, no. 41 (April-June, 1961) 124-125.

Hallelujah Anyway

K204. Spector, R.D. *Saturday Review of Literature* L, 6 (February 11, 1967) 40.

K205. Cushman, Jerome. *Library Journal* XCII (February 15, 1967) 781.

K206. *Virginia Quarterly Review* XLIII, 3 (Summer 1967) 111.

K207. Roseliep, Raymond. "Our Land and Our Sea and Hallelujah." *Poetry* CVII (December 1967) 193-194.

Love and War Poems

K208.   Cunliffe, David. "Raging Thunderbolts of Peace Re-
         visited." *Peace News*, no. 1988 (February 7, 1975) 10-11.

But Even So

K209.   Greenwald, John. " 'Picture Poetry' Grips the Reader."
         Minneapolis (MN) *Star* (February 11, 1969).

Collected Poems

K210.   Schneider, Duane. *Library Journal* XCIII (May 1, 1968)
         1906.
K211.   *Chicago Tribune* (August 6, 1968) 16.
K212.   Howes, Victor. *Christian Science Monitor* (October 11,
         1968) 11.
K213.   Packard, William. *New York Times Book Review* (Oc-
         tober 20, 1968) 20.
K214.   *Choice* V (October 1968) 958.
K215.   Walsh, Chad. *Book World* (November 3, 1968) 20.
K216.   Kessler, James. "Caged Sybil." *Saturday Review of Liter-
         ture* LI, 50 (December 14, 1968) 34-36.

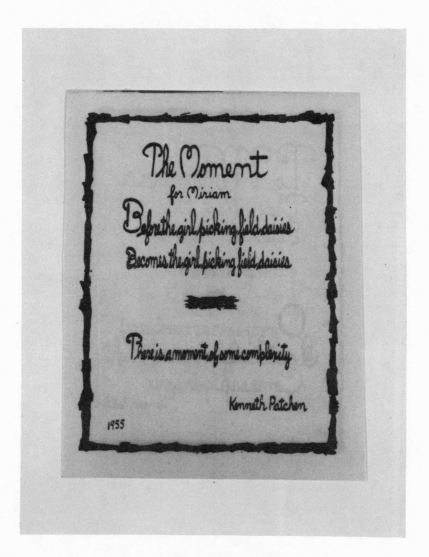

First Leaf of *The Moment* (1960). A30.

Title Page of *But Even So* (1968). A35a.

L 1. *University of California, Los Angeles.* Department of Special Collections, University Research Library.

Letters from Kenneth Patchen to Kenneth Roxroth
April 29, 1948 TLS 1p. Old Lyme, Connecticut
June 11, 1948 TLS 1p. Old Lyme
July 10, 1948 TLS 2p. Old Lyme
August 5, 1948 TLS 1p. Old Lyme
August 14, 1948 TLS 1p. Old Lyme
October 3, [1948] TLS 1p. Old Lyme
February 19, 1949 TLS 1p. n.p. [Old Lyme]
February 6, 1950 ALS 2p. Old Lyme
February 7, 1950 ALS 1p. n.p. [Old Lyme]
February 12, 1950 ALS 1p. n.p. [Old Lyme]
February 12, [1951] TLS 2p. Old Lyme
October 15, 1951 ALS 2p. n.p. [Old Lyme]
January 19, 1956 ALS 2p. Palo Alto, California
July 26, [1956] ALS 1p. Palo Alto Hospital 350 El Camino Real
January 26, [1957] TLS 1p. 852 Bryant St., Palo Alto
November 4, 1957 TLS 2p. 2340 Sierra Court, Palo Alto
no date TLS sp. n.p.

Letters from Kenneth Patchen to Henry Miller
July 25, [1941] ALS 2p. 81 Bleecker Street, New York City
December 27, 1945 ALS 1p. 336 West 12th St., NYC
January 18, [1946] ALS 2p. 336 West 12th St.
January 21, [1946] ALS 2p. 336 West 12th St.
March 9, 1946 ALS 1p. 336 West 12th St.
April 2, 1946 ALS 2p. 336 West 12th St.
April 27, 1946 ALS 2p. 336 West 12th St.
June 22, 1946 ALS 2p. 336 West 12th St.
July 14, 1946 ALS 1p. Mount Pleasant, New York
August 4, 1946 ALS 1p. Mount Pleasant
November 13, 1946 ALS 2p. 336 West 12th St., NYC
January 8, 1948 ALS 1p. Old Lyme, Connecticut
March 1, 1949 TLS 2p. Old Lyme
November 6, 1949 ALS 1p. Old Lyme
October 23, [1949] ALS 2p. Old Lyme

February 1, 1950 TLS 1p. Old Lyme
March 28, [1950] ALS 4p. Old Lyme
May 31, 1950 ALS 2p. n.p. [Old Lyme]
July 9, 1950 ALS 2p. Old Lyme
July 30, 1951 ANS 1p. Old Lyme
June 26, 1952 TLS 1p. 377 Green Street, San Francisco
September 15, 1956 ALS 1p. 852 Bryant Street, Palo Alto
February 27, 1957 TLS 1p. 852 Bryant Street
March 6, 1957 TLS p. n.p.
March 10, [1957] TLS 1p. 2340 Sierra Court, Palo Alto
n.d. 1961 ANS 2p. 2340 Sierra Court
January 15, 1962 ALS 6p. 2340 Sierra Court
Miriam Patchen to HM, n.d. [1950] ALS 1p. n.p.
Miriam Patchen to HM, n.d. [1950] ALS 3p. n.p.

Miller's Manuscript of *Patchen: Man of Anger and Light*, 26 leaves (holograph and typescript) with manuscript corrections in pencil by Patchen

Patchen's original manuscript for his contribution to *The Happy Rock*, 1 leaf, holograph

Three letters to Bern Porter, 1944-1945.

L 2.   *University of California, Santa Cruz.* The Kenneth Patchen Archive, Special Collections, The University Library.

Manuscripts:
The Journal of Albion Moonlight. 135 loose pages, with some leaves of varying sizes; three notebooks of various sizes. In box made by Miriam Patchen, with a label painted by Kenneth Patchen. All in holograph.
Sleepers Awake. Loose sheets and notebooks, in holograph, in box made by Miriam Patchen, with label handwritten by Kenneth Patchen; typescripts; complete galley and page proofs, annotated for printer.
Selected Poems, 1946. Galley proofs.
They Keep Riding Down All the Time. Originals of cover drawings.
Don't Look Now. Holograph ms. written on yellow paper in a "Big Chief" tablet measuring 42 x 30 cm.; typescript.
Poemscapes. Complete manuscript, typescript, and page proofs.

Hurrah for Anything. Manuscript, originals of drawings.
The Famous Boating Party. Typescript and make-up dummy.
Collected Poems. Manuscript, corrected typescripts, proofs.
Glory Never Guesses. Holograph ms. of text, silkscreen originals.
A Surprise for the Bagpipe Player. Holograph ms. of text, silkscreen originals.
Aflame & Afun of Walking Faces. Originals of illustrations, page proofs.
Wonderings. Originals of drawings.

Letters from James Laughlin to Kenneth Patchen
Approximately 200 letters covering the period 1949-1972.

Principal Works
Copies of each of Patchen's works in all editions, including most foreign translations, and each of the recordings, and the unique copy of *In Peaceable Caves* (A19).

Six scrapbooks, kept by Kenneth and Miriam Patchen for the years 1934-1963, containing reviews and other press notices, transcripts of letters commenting on Patchen's work, and general clippings.

All of the papier-mache sculptures Patchen made in his lifetime, ca. 1960-1970. Six exist; each is an imaginary animal.

Ephemera including all items noted in the miscellanea section of the bibliography, as well as over one hundred additional newspaper clippings, catalogs listing Patchen books, posters advertising his poetry-and-jazz appearances and poetry readings, pens, brushes, and other materials of his painting-poems, advertisements, flyers, slides, photographs, etc.

The collection, which was purchased from Mrs. Miriam Patchen, the author's widow, in 1975, is as yet uncatalogued.

L 3. *University of Chicago*, Special Collections, The Joseph Regenstein Library.

Amy Bonner Papers, Box 2.
KP to Amy Bonner, April 10, 1940 ALS 1p. 81 Bleeker St., NYC

KP to AB, May 20, 1940 ALS 1p. 81 Bleeker St.

Poetry Magazine Papers, 1912-1936, Box 37, Folder 4.

KP to Harriet Monroe, April 10, 1933 ALS 2p. Manumit School, Pauling, New York

KP to HM, May 20, 1933 ALS 3p. 228 West 13th St., NYC

KP to HM, September 4, 1933 ALS 1p. c/o John Parke, Hanover, New Hampshire

KP to HM, April 17, 1934 ALS 1p. Edgehill Drive, Warren, Ohio

KP to HM, May 31, 1934 ALS 1p. Edgehill Drive

KP to Morton Dauwen Zabel, August 17, 1934 ALS 1p. Warren, Ohio

KP to MDZ, November 13, 1934 TLS 1p. 20 Bullfinch St., Boston, Mass.

KP to MDZ, June 5, 1935 ALS 1p. Rhinebeck, New York

KP to HM, n.d. ALS 1p. 1204 Fulton Ave., Bonx, N.Y. "Empty Dwelling Places", "Tristanesque", "Parting Coney Island." Corrected page proofs of three preceding poems.

Poetry Magazine Papers, 1936-1953 (Series I), Box 19, Folder 11.

KP to MDZ, September 10, 1936 TLS 1p. 3 Placita Rafaela, Santa Fe, New Mexico

KP, Biography, July 23, 1939 ALS 1p. Concord, Mass.

KP to *Poetry* editors, May 26, n.y. ALS 1p. 317 West 4th St., NYC

KP to George Dillon, September 30, 1942 ALS 1p. 317 West 4th St.

KP to *Poetry* editors, July 9, 1948 TLS 1p. Old Lyme, Connecticut

KP to Marion Strobel, August 29, 1948 TLS 1p. Old Lyme

KP to Karl Shapiro, July 31, 1951 ALS 1p. Old Lyme

KP to KS, July 23, 1952 TLS 1p. 377 Green Street, San Francisco

KP to KS, August 8, 1952 ALS 1p. 377 Green Street

KP to KS, September 4, 1952 ALS 1p. 377 Green Street

The Kenneth Patchen Fund Announcement (W.H. Auden, T.S. Eliot, Archibald Macleish, and Thorton Wilder). 1p.

An Evening of Poetry . . . for the benefit of . . . Kenneth Patchen, Saturday April 14. 11.

Miriam Patchen to Mrs. Shapiro, February 4, n.y. 2p. Old Lyme

Kenneth Patchen, printed list of publications. 6p.

"Egypt," "Attila," "So When She Lay Beside Me," "But of Life?," "Beautiful You are," "The Unanswering Correspondences," "All is Safe . . .," "Under a Tree," "The Stages of Narcissus," "To the Memory of Robert Shelley;" all typescripts.

Poetry Magazine Papers, 1954-1961, Box 27, Folder 4.

"Wide, Wide in the Rose's Side," "the Great Birds," "O She is as Lovely—Often," "And Tallness Stood Upon the Sky Like a Sparkling Mane," "First Came the Lion-Rider," "O Now the Drenched Land Wakes," "Poemscape;" all typescripts.

Poetry Magazine Papers, 1954-1961, Box 27, Folder 5.

KP to Henry Rago, October 6, 1955 TLS 1p. 377 Green Street, San Francisco

KP to HR, November 7, 1955 TLS 1p. 377 Green Street (with ad for *Glory Never Guesses* attached).

KP to HR, November 18, 1955 TLS 1p. 377 Green Street

HR to KP, December 7, 1956 ALS 1p.

KP to HR, May 9, 1956 TLS 1p. 852 Bryant St., Palo Alto

HR to KP, May 11, 1956 L 1p.

KP to HR, May 15, 1956 TLS 1p. 852 Bryant St.

KP to HR, May 23, 1956 TLS 2p. 852 Bryant St.

HR to KP, June 11, 1956 L 1p.

KP to HR, August 29, 1956 ALS 1p. 852 Bryant St.

HR to KP, September 10, 1956 L 1p.

KP to HR, February 22, 1957 TLS 1p. 852 Bryant St.

HR to KP, March 12, 1957 L 2p.

KP to HR, March 26, 1957 TLS 1p. 2340 Sierra Court, Palo Alto

KP to HR, April 11, 1957 TLS 1p. 2340 Sierra Court

KP to HR, April 26, 1957 TLS 1p. 2340 Sierra Court

HR to KP, April 29, 1957 L 2p.

KP to HR, August 12, 1957 TLS 1p. 2340 Sierra Court

KP to HR, August 13, 1957 postcard 2340 Sierra Court

HR to KP, August 27, 1957 L 1p.

KP to HR, October 17, 1957 ALS 1p. 2340 Sierra Court

HR to KP, October 21, 1957 L 1p.

KP to HR, October 27, 1957 TLS 2p. 2340 Sierra Court

HR to KP, November 21, 1957 L 1p.
A Statement by Kenneth Patchen, October 26, 1957.
KP to HR, December 4, 1957 TLS 1p. 2340 Sierra Court
(with clipping attached).
Miriam Patchen to HR, 1957 ALS 3p. 2340 Sierra Court
Miriam Patchen to HR, 1957 ALS 2p. 2340 Sierra Court
HR to KP, July 25, 1958 L 1p. (press release attached).
HR to KP, September 10, 1958 L 1p.
KP to HR, August 15, 1958 TLS 2p. 2340 Sierra Court
(with hand-painted envelope).
HR to Miriam Patchen, August 24, 1959 L 1p.
HR to Miriam and Kenneth Patchen, March 20, 1959 L 1p.
KP to HR, May 6, 1959 ALS 1p. 2340 Sierra Court
HR to KP, May 11, 1959 L 1p.
Miriam Patchen to HR, July 14, 1959 TLS 1p. 2340 Sierra
Court
MP to HR, 1959 TLS 1p. 2340 Sierra Court
MP to HR, February 15, 1959 TLS 1p. 2340 Sierra Court
MP to HR, 1959 TLS 1p. 2340 Sierra Court
KP to HR, February 6, 1960 TLS 2p. 2340 Sierra Court
HR to KP, February 24, 1960 L 1p.
Copy for Picture Poems Advertisement
KP to HR, October 27, 1960 ALS 2p. 2340 Sierra Court
HR to KP, April 28, 1961 L 1p.

Secretary, *Poetry* magazine to Mrs. Guernsey Van Riper,
Jr., April 28, 1961 L 1p.

MP to John Nims, May 29, n.y. TLS 1p. (Enclosed, William L. Rothenberg of Carnegie Fund for Authors, to
William Packard, May 9, 1961 L 1p.).

Two Poems for Christmas by Kenneth Patchen, Christmas
card to HR, 1958.

Christmas card, n.d., signed Miriam and Kenneth Patchen.

L 4.   *Harvard University*, Special Collections, Houghton
Library

Letters from Kenneth Patchen to Edward Estlin Cummings.
June 4, 1941 ALS 1p. 81 Bleecker Street, NYC
January 13, 1942 ANS 1p. 265 Avenue A, NYC
January 28, 1942 ALS 1p. n.p.
May 15, 1944 ANS 1p. Concord, Mass.

March 28, 1950 ACS 1p. Oly Lyme, Conn.
September 4, [1952] ALS 2p. 377 Green St., San Francisco
September 18, [1952] ALS 1p. 377 Green Street
March 10, 1953 TLS 1p. 377 Green Street
May 10, 1953 TLS 1p. 377 Green Street
May 27, 1953 ALS 1p. 377 Green Street
June 19, 1953 ALS 1p. 377 Green Street
July 31, 1953 TLS 1p. 377 Green Street
October, 1954 Telegram 1p. 377 Green Street
April 9, 1955 ALS 1p. 377 Green Street
May 2, 1955 TLS 1p. n.p. [377 Green Street]
September 26, 1955 ALS 1p. 377 Green Street
December 7, 1955 TLS 1p. 377 Green Street
March 4, 1956 ALS 1p. 852 Bryant Street, Palo Alto
May 8, 1956 TLS 2p. 852 Bryant Street
June 20, [1956] ALS 2p. Palo Alto Hospital, 350 El Ca-
    mino Real
July 23, [1956] ALS 2p. Palo Alto Hospital, 350 El Ca-
    mino Real
February 27, [1957] TLS 2p. 852 Bryant Street, Palo Alto
March 10, [1957] TLS 1p. 2340 Sierra Court, Palo Alto
April 10, 1957 TLS 1p. 2340 Sierra Court
November 25, 1958 TLS 1p. 2340 Sierra Court
March 6, 1959 ALS 2p. 2340 Sierra Court
January 1, 1960 ALS 2p. 2340 Sierra Court
May 30, 1962 Postcard Mount Zion Hospital
July 30, n.y. ALS 1p. Old Lyme, Conn.
August 4, n.y. ALS 2p. Old Lyme

Letters from Edward Estlin Cummings to Kenneth
    Patchin
August 26, 1942 TLS 1p.
May 19, 1953 TLS 1p.
April 18, 1955 TLS 1p.
January 18, 1958 TLS 1p.
Four letters (TLS), no date 4p.

Other letters
KP to Sherry Mangan, March 26, 1938 ALS 1p. 5526½
    Virginia Ave., Los Angeles, CA
KP to SM, May 13, 1942 ALS 1p. 265 Avenue A, NYC
SM to KP, 1942 ALS 1p.

KP to Thomas Wolfe, April 1937 TLS 1p. 1414 North Las
Palmas, Hollywood, CA
Printed letter from Patchen's doctor, reporting on
Patchen's condition, March 10, 1955 1p.

L 5.   *Huntington Library* San Marino, California

Kenneth Patchen to Wallace Stevens
April 18, 1941 ALS 3p. 81 Bleecker St., NYC

April 23, 1941 ALS 1p. 81 Bleecker St.
June 2, 1941 ALS 2p. 81 Bleecker St.
June 4, 1941 ALS 1p. 81 Bleecker St.
December 22, 1941 ALS 1p. 265 Avenue A, NYC
April 2, [1941] ALS 2p. n.p.
n.d. [1941] ANS 1p. n.p.
November 5, 1942 TLS 1p. 317 West 4th St., NYC
November 16, 1943 ALS 1p. 331 West 22nd St., NYC

Miriam Patchen to Wallac Stevens
March 25, 1941 ALS 4p. 81 Bleecker St.
n.d. [1941] ANS 4p. n.p.
n.d. [1941] ANS 1p. 81 Bleecker St.

Miriam and Kenneth Patchen to Wallace Stevens
December 20, 1944 ANS 1p. n.p.

Wallace Stevens to Kenneth Patchen
April 19, 1941 TLS 1p.
June 3, 1941 TLS 1p.
June 5, 1941 TLS 1p.
November 9, 1942 TLS 1p.
November 16, 1942 TLS 1p.
March 28, 1941 TLS 1p.

L 6.   *Indiana University*, Special Collections, The Lilly Library.

From Kenneth Patchen to Harry Redl
March 2, 1956 TLS 1p. 852 Bryant Street, Palo Alto
March 23, 1956 Postcard Palo Alto, CA
March 29, 1956 Postcard 377 Green St., San Francisco
February 18, 1959 Postcard Vancouver, Canada
June 15, n.y. ALS 1p. 2340 Sierra Court, Palo Alto
Two letters, no dates. Palo Alto, CA

From Kenneth Patchen to Louis Untermeyer
August 3, 1941 ALS 1p. 81 Bleecker St., NYC
August 13, 1941 TLS 1p. 81 Bleecker St.
February 28, 1947 TLS 1p. Old Lyme, Conn.
March 4, 1947 ALS 1p. Old Lyme
August 11, 1947 TLS 1p. Old Lyme
March 17, 1949 ALS 1p. Old Lyme

From Miriam Patchen to David Anton Randall
August 6, 1945
August 30, 1965

From Miriam Patchen to Louis Untermeyer
October 13, 1949

About Kenneth Patchen
James Laughlin to Louis Untermeyer, October 25, 1949
Hiram Patchen to Louis Untermeyer, n.d.
Louis Untermeyer to Pearson, October 25, 1949 (carbon).
The Kenneth Patchen Fund Announcement (W.H. Augen,
T.S. Eliot, Archibald MacLeish, and Thornton Wilder).

L 7. *State University of New York at Buffalo*, Poetry Collection, The University Libraries.

Manuscripts
"As She Was Thus Alone In the Clear Moonlight." Typed
version with varied titles.
"The Black Panther and the Little Boy." Corrected version
in pencil.
"Crop Menace." Corrected copy in pencil.
"Footnotes to a Nightmare." Corrected version in pencil.
From "The Argument (Hunted City)." Corrected version
in pencil, two versions os second part.
"He is Guarded by Crowds and Shackled by Formalities."
Two copies in pencil, with different titles.
"I Here Deliver You My Will and Testament." Corrected
version in pencil.
Long titles from *First Will and Testament*. Corrected
version in pencil.
Notebook. Drawings and poems in pencil, text published
in *Cloth of the Tempest*.
"Outside Looking Outside." Corrected version in pencil.

"Poem Written After Reading Certain Poets Sired By the
English School and Bitched By the C.P." Corrected
version in pencil.

Manuscript sheet (listed as "possibily . . . rec'd in *The
Illiterati.*") "Stop Me If You've Heard This One."
Corrected version in pencil.

Cloth of the Tempest. Publisher's dummy.

L 8.   *Northwestern University.* Special Collections.

Letters from Kenneth Patchen to Jasper Wood
January 7, 1944 APS 1p. 336 West 12th St., NYC
March 11, [1944] TLS 1p. 336 West 12th St.
April 21, [1944] APS 1p. 336 West 12th St.
September 12, 1944 ALS 2p. 336 West 12th St.
September 21, 1944 TLS 1p. 336 West 12th St.
September 23, [1944] TLS 1p. 336 West 12th St.
October 2, [1944] TLS 2p. 336 West 12th St.
November 3, 1944 TLS 1p. 336 West 12th St.
November 30, 1944 TLS 2p. 336 West 12th St.
December 24, 1944 TLS 2p. 336 West 12th St.
December 30, 1944 APS 1p. 336 West 12th St.
January 3, 1945 TLS 1p. 336 West 12th St.
February 24, 1945 APS 1p. 336 West 12th St.
December 27, 1945 ALS 1p. 336 West 12th St.
January 5, 1946 ALS 1p. 336 West 12th St.
January 18, [1946?] ALS 2p. 336 West 12th St.
February 12, [1946?] ALS 1p. 336 West 12th St.
February 28, [1946?] ALS 2p. 336 West 12th St.
March 19, 1946 ALS 1p. 336 West 12th St.
April 3, 1946 ALS 1p. 336 West 12th St.
April 17, [1946] ALS 1p. 336 West 12th St.
May 16, [1946?] ALS 1p. 336 West 12th St.
May 30, [1946?] ALS 1p. 336 West 12th St.
June 10, [1946?] ALS 1p. 336 West 12th St.
June 13, [1946?] ALS 2p. 336 West 12th St.
June 22, [1946?] ALS 1p. 336 West 12th St.
July 15, 1946 ALS 1p. Mount Pleasant, New York
August 5, 1946 APS 1p. Mount Pleasant
September 4, 1946 ALS 1p. 336 West 12th St., NYC
July 28, 1947 ALS 2p. Old Lyme, Conn.
August 19, 1947 APS 1p. Old Lyme
October 24, 1947 ALS 1p. Old Lyme

November 4, 1947 ALS 1p. Old Lyme
November 8, 1947 ALS 1p. Old Lyme
December 31, 1947 ALS 2p. Old Lyme
June 28, 1948 TLS 1p. Old Lyme
January 17, 1949 APS 1p. Old Lyme
February 6, 1950 ALS 2p. Old Lyme

Miriam Patchen to Jasper Wood
n.d. [1944-6] ALS 1p.

Letters from Miriam Patchen to Jon and Louise (Gypsy)
  Webb
to J&LW n.d. TLS 1p. 2340 Sierra Court, Palo Alto
to ? [JW] n.d. ALS 1p. 2340 Sierra Court
to J&LW n.d. ALS 2p. 2340 Sierra Court
to J&LW n.s. APS 1p. 2340 Sierra Court
to J&LW n.d. ALS 1p. 2340 Sierra Court
to J&LW n.d. ACS (incomplete) 1p. 2340 Sierra Court
to J&LW n.d. TLS 2p. 2340 Sierra Court
to J&LW n.d. TLS 2p. 2340 Sierra Court
to J&LW n.d. (Christmas) ACS 1p. 2340 Sierra Court
to J&LW n.d. APS 1p. 2340 Sierra Court
to J&LW n.d. APS 1p. 2340 Sierra Court
to JW August 22, 1962 ALS 2p. 2340 Sierra Court
to JW September 11, 1962 ALS 3p. 2340 Sierra Court
to JW September 23, 1962 ALS 2p. 2340 Sierra Court
to JW October 7, 1962 ALS 1p. 2340 Sierra Court
to J&LW December 2, [1962] ALS 2p. 2340 Sierra Court
to J&LW 1962 Christmas Card 1p. 2340 Sierra Court
to J&LW 1962 TLS 1p. 2340 Sierra Court
to J&LW February 2, 1963 ALS 2p. 2340 Sierra Court
to J&LW April, 1963 APS 1p. 2340 Sierra Court
to J&LW July 23, 1963 TLS 2p. 2340 Sierra Court
to J&LW August 3, [1963] ACS 2p. 2340 Sierra Court
to J&LW August 27, 1963 ALS 2p. 2340 Sierra Court
to J&LW September 9, 1963 APS 1p. 2340 Sierra Court
to J&LW October 16, 1963 ALS 2p. 2340 Sierra Court
to J&LW October 22, 1963 ALS 1p. 2340 Sierra Court
to J&LW October 23, 1963 ALS 2p. 2340 Sierra Court
to J&LW November 5, 1963 ALS 1p. 2340 Sierra Court
to J&LW December 19, 1963 ACS 1p. 2340 Sierra Court
to J&LW March 4, 1964 ALS 1p. c/o David Glover
  112 Garcia Avenue, San Leandro, CA
to J&LW April 2, 1964 APS 1p. 2340 Sierra Court

to J&LW April 26, 1964 TLS 2p. 2340 Sierra Court
to J&LW April 27, 1964 ALS 2p. 2340 Sierra Court
to J&LW May 13, 1964 APS 2p. 2340 Sierra Court
to J&LW July 7, 1964 APCS 1p. 2340 Sierra Court
to J&LW July 12, 1964 ALS 2p. 2340 Sierra Court
to J&LW October 8, 1964 APCS 1p. 2340 Sierra Court
to J&LW December 26, 1964 ALS 1p. 2340 Sierra Court
to J&LW 1964 TLS 1p. 2340 Sierra Court
to LW March 24, 1965 APS 1p. 2340 Sierra Court
to J&LW June 19, 1965 AP 1p. 2340 Sierra Court
to J&LW July 30, 1965 APS 1p. 2340 Sierra Court
to J&LW August 28, 1965 APS 1p. 2340 Sierra Court
to J&LW May 30, 1966 ALS 6p. 2340 Sierra Court
to J&LW August 18, 1966 ALS 1p. 2340 Sierra Court
to J&LW February 19, 1967 ALS 2p. 2340 Sierra Court
to J&LW April 14, 1967 APS 1p. 2340 Sierra Court
to J&LW April, 1967 APS 1p. 2340 Sierra Court
to JW May 1, 1967 APS 1p. 2340 Sierra Court
to J&LW May 11, 1967 APS 1p. 2340 Sierra Court
to J&LW July 22, 1967 APS 1p. 2340 Sierra Court
to J&LW August 7, 1967 APS 2p. 2340 Sierra Court
to J&LW August 30, 1967 APS 1p. 2340 Sierra Court
to J&LW September 10, 1967 ALS 4p. 2340 Sierra Court
to J&LW September 19, 1967 APS 1p. 2340 Sierra Court
to J&LW December 18, 1967 Christmas Card 1p. 2340
    Sierra Court
to J&LW January 22, 1968 ALS 5p. 2340 Sierra Court
yo J&LW March 12, 1968 APS 1p. 2340 Sierra Court
to J&LW June 7, 1968 ALS 2p. 2340 Sierra Court
to J&LW December 25, 1968 Christmas Card 1p. 2340
    Sierra Court
to J&LW March 2, 1969 ALS 1p. 2340 Sierra Court
Kenneth Patchen to Jon Webb November 15, 1963 Tele-
    gram 1p.
Kenneth and Miriam Patchen to J&LW August 4, 1968
    Telegram 1p.
Jon Webb to Miriam and Kenneth Patchen August 24,
    1963 TL (carbon) 1p.
JW to M&KP June 10, 1965 TLS 2p.

Manuscripts
"The Panel of First Love and Its Dark Wonderful Lesson."
    On notebook paper. 9 1.

Pencil figures on notebook paper. 8 1.
"The City Wears a Slouch Hat." Radio Play. Typescript,
22 1.

Ephemera
Originals of items in the *Outsider* 4/5 tribute to Patchen.

L 9. *University of Pennsylvania.* Charles Patterson Van Pelt
Library.

Letters from Kenneth Patchen to James T. Farrell
March 22, [1934] TLS 1p. 21 Bank Street, New York City
April 29, 1937 TLS 1p. 1414 North Las Palmas, Holly-
wood, CA
July 24, [1937] ALS 1p. 2163½ Beechwood Terrace,
Hollywood, CA
September 25, 1937 TLS 1p. 2163½ Beechwood Terrace
November 18, [1937] ALS 1p. 2163½ Beechwood Terrace
March 21, 1938 ALS 1p. 5526½ Virginia Avenue, Los
Angeles, CA
June 14, 1938 ALS 2p. 5526½ Virginia Avenue
February 3, 1939 ALS 2p. 427 South Figueroa, Los
Angeles, CA

L10. *Princeton University.* Firestone Library, R.P. Blackmur
Archive.

Three letters from Kenneth Patchen to R.P. Blackmur.
No other information available.

L11. *University of Texas as Austin*, Humanities Research
Center.

Letters From Kenneth Patchen
to Christopher Morley, January 26, 1941 ALS 1p. 81
Bleecker St., NYC
to Wrey Gardiner, January 6, 1947 APCS Old Lyme,
Conn.
to CM, February 28, 1947 TLS 1p. Old Lyme
to CM, August 11, 1947 TLS 1p. Old Lyme
to Charles Norman, December 8, 1947 APCS Old Lyme
to Dame Edith Sitwell, September 26, 1950 ALS 1p.
Old Lyme
to Julian Beck, April 6, 1959 ALS n.p. Old Lyme

to William J. and Lillian Perlman 9ALS 2TLS, 3 Christmas cards with notes

Letters To Kenneth Patchen
From Christopher Morley, March 7, 1947 TccL
From Julian Beck, March 26, 1960 TccL

Manuscripts
Tccms sent to Terence I.F. Armstrong (agent), 31pp.
(poems).
Bound proof copy of *See You In The Morning.*
Bound book of Arms poems from *The Dark Kingdom,
Teeth of the Lion,* and *Cloth of the Tempest.*
Paste-up proof copy of *Sleepers Awake.*

L12.   *Yale University,* Collection of American Literature,
Beinecke Rare Book and Manuscript Library.

Letters From Kenneth Patchen
to Harry Roskolenko, March 26, 1938 ALS 1p. 5526½ Virginia Avenue, Los Angeles
to HR, December 21, 1938 TLS 1p. 427 South Figueroa
St., Los Angeles
to HR, January 16, 1939 TLS 1p. 427 South Figueroa St.
to HR, February 9, 1939 ALS 1p. 427 South Figueroa St.
to HR, July 17, 1939 ANS 2p. Concord, Mass.
to HR, August 5, [1939] ANS 1p. Norfolk, Conn.
to William Carlos Williams, November 16, 1939 TLS 1p.
Norfolk, Conn.
to HR, December 8, 1939 TLS 1p. Norfolk, Conn.
to Carl Van Vechten, August 10, 1941 APCS 1p. 81
Bleecker St., NYC
to T.C. Wilson, 24 March n.y. TLS 1p. 21 Bank St., NYC
to TCW, October 7, n.y. ALS 1p. 1204 Fulton Ave.,
Bronx, New York
to TCW, n.d. ALS 1p. Edgehill Drive, Warren, Ohio

I have included here items in two categories: 1. those in which
Kenneth or Miriam Patchen had a direct part, and which do not
fit into any other categories in the larger bibliography, and 2. an-
nouncements of Patchen's books, whether or not he had respon-
sibility for the item itself.

M 1. *The Echoes, 1929.* 1 blank leaf, 3 leaves [7]-[86] p., 13
leaves, 1 blank leaf. 28 x 20.5 cm. Black plastic with
raised lettering. The yearbook of Warren G. Harding
High School, Warren, Ohio, which Patchen attended
from 1926 to 1929. He was editor of the yearbook in
1929, the year of his graduation.

M 2. *"First Will & Testament* . . . will be published November
7th by New Directions at $2.50." Book announcement.
Broadside. 23 x 15.5 cm. White paper.

M 3. "The Journal of Albion Moonlight." Announcement and
order form for the private edition (1941). Written by
the Patchens, giving Miriam's name and their home
address for orders, and used by them as a mailout.
4p. [one folded sheet 20.5 x 25 cm.] 20.5 x 12.5 cm. White
paper.

M 4. "The House of Harriss & Givens announces the publication
of their first book." Announcement and order form for
The Dark Kingdom. 4p. [one folded sheet 21 x 25.5
cm.] 21 x 12.5 cm. White paper.

M 5. "Journal of Albion Moonlight." 8.5 x 14 cm. Postcard.
White with green design and black lettering. Advertisement for the United Book Guild edition.

M 6. "Arthur Sturcke & David Ruff." Christmas exhibition
of Paintings at the Washington Square Gallery (New
York City) December 7th to 30th 1945. 4p. [one folded
sheet 23 x 32 cm.] 23 x 16 cm. White paper. The second
page of this guide to the exhibition is a testimonial to
the two artists by Patchen.

M 7. Padell announcement for *Sleepers Awake*, with order
form. Broadside. 26 x 18 cm. White paper. Patchen was
intimately involved in every stage of the preparation,
layout, and printing of the book, including this
announcement.

M 8.   "Announcing a Special Limited Edition." [Advertisement
        for the limited edition of *Sleepers Awake*]. 4p. One sheet,
        23 x 31 cm., folded once to 23 x 15.5 cm. Yellow with
        black lettering. Written by Patchen and carrying Miriam
        Patchen's name and their address for orders.

M 9.   Padell advertisement for *Sleepers Awake* and *The Journal
        of Albion Moonlight*. 14 x 8.5 cm. Postcard. White with
        red lettering (some are white with blue and red lettering).

M10.   "Kenneth Patchen. A First Bibliography." Compiled by
        Gail Eaton [Miriam Patchen]. 4p. [One folded sheet].
        18 x 13 cm. White paper. A listing of Patchen's first
        fourteen books.

M11.   "Kenneth Patchen." A printed list of his books, prepared
        by him and Miriam, with appropriate quotes from
        reviews. 6p. [one sheet 21.5 x 32 cm., folded across in
        two places] 21.5 x 14 cm. White paper. With a photo-
        graph of Patchen by Robin Carson.

M12.   "Kenneth Patchen/Books From Padell." 4p. One sheet
        20.5 x 28 cm., folded once to 20.5 x 14 cm. White with
        black lettering. Listing of the nine books by Patchen
        which Padell published, with an order blank. Portrait
        of Patchen on front.

M13.   Padell advertisement for *See You in the Morning*. 4p.
        15.5 x 17.5 cm., folded once to 15.5 x 9 cm. Grey paper
        with green lettering.

M14.   The Print Workshop, announcement for *Orchards,
        Thrones & Caravans*. 4p. [one folded sheet, printed
        only on one side] 9.5 x 24 cm. White paper.

M15.   Jargon announcement for *Fables and Other Little Tales*.
        4p. 11 x 15 cm. Yellow paper.

M16.   "For Sale 2 New Painted Edition Patchen Books." 50 x
        16 cm., folded twice to 16.5 x 16 cm. Heavy white paper
        with black and red lettering. Advertisement written
        by Patchen for the painted book editions of *The Famous
        Boating Party* and *Fables and Other Little Tales*, giving
        his home address in Palo Alto for orders.

M17.   *Glory Never Guesses* announcement and order form.
        Broadside. 47.5 x 18 cm. Special white paper. Written
        by Patchen, and carrying his home address for orders.

M18.   *Surprise for the Bagpipe Player* announcement and order
        form. Broadside. 15 x 21 cm. On special paper in two
        issues, blue and brown, both laid with bits of silver

paper. Written by Patchen and carrying his home
address for orders.

M19. "Kenneth Patchen Reads With The Chamber Jazz Sextet."
4 p. [one sheet 30.5 x 45.5 cm., folding to 30.5 x 23 cm.
text, and further to 15 x 23 cm. to expose title]. Record
enclosure. White paper.

M20. "Hurrah for Anything." 21.4 x 14 cm. White paper with
purple lettering. Book announcement.

M21. "Kenneth Patchen." Program notes for a reading at The
Poetry Center at San Francisco State College, written
by Gail Eaton [Miriam Patchen]. Two typed sheets,
stapled. 28 x 21.5 cm. White bond. List of books and
biographical notes.

M22. "I am offering for sale 3 new Painted Books [*When We
Were Here Together, Hurrah for Anything*, and *Poemscapes*]." Broadside. 35.5 x 21.5 cm. White paper.
Written by Patchen, printed in his hand, and used by
him as a mailout.

M23. "Don't Look Now." Program for first performance at The
Troupe Theatre in Palo Alto, California. [9] p. 16 x 12
cm. Red paper with white design. Gives information on
Patchen and the play, a list of the players, and a brief
bibliography of Patchen's works.

M24a. "pomes penyeach 1959." Ten Poems by Kenneth Patchen
(Plus three Prose Excerpts). 4p. 43 x 28.5 cm. [one folded
sheet 43 x 57 cm.]. Newsprint. Edited by John Wittwer
from previously published poems. Printed in Seattle,
Washington. Includes statements and quotes from reviews as well as a listing, with prices, of Patchen's books.
"Headline" reads "Patchen and Jazz." Used to advertise
Patchen's poetry-and-jazz readings in Seattle and Vancouver in 1959 and sold at the readings for 10¢.

M24b. Second Printing. Identified as such under title. Identical
except deletes advertisement for reading on lower half of
first page.

M25. "San Francisco Tribute to Kenneth Patchen." Program
held January 29, 1961 to raise funds for treatments of
Patchen's illness. 8p. 14 x 20.5 cm. Handbound with red
threads, and carrying a holograph poem and drawing
by Patchen. White paper.

M26. Nantahala Foundation announcement for *But Even So*.
Intended to be Jargon #50, produced in three editions,

but was never published by them. Tipped-in reproduction, "a fragment of plate 1 from *But Even So*." 4p. [one sheet 30.5 x 46 cm., printed on one side and folded twice]. 23 x 15.5 cm. Tan paper.

M27.   "Paintings by Kenneth Patchen," exhibit at City Lights Gallery March-April 1965. 4p. [one folded sheet, printed on only one side]. 20.5 x 14 cm. White paper. On the back is a previously unpublished drawing by Patchen.

M28.   Announcement for the record *Patchen's Funny Fables*. Postcard. 8.5 x 14 cm. White with black lettering and a picture in red of the "celery flute player" by Patchen.

Title Page Spread of *Don't Look Now* (1977). A43a.

Collage.

CROSS-REFERENCED INDEX

The Index listings are divided into two parts:

Part One (*By Patchen*): Sections A-G, L (material by or letters from Kenneth Patchen or from Miriam Patchen acting for Patchen), and M.

Part Two (*About Patchen*): Sections H-K, and L (material about or letters to Patchen).

Material about Patchen included in editions of his work is indexed in both parts.

Four categories of information are listed, differentiated as follows:

Separate titles (e.g. books, pamphlets, plays, musical compositions) are in all capital letters.

Other titles (e.g., individual poems, stories, significant section headings) are in quotation marks.

Names of periodicals are in italics.

Other names and entities (e.g., editors, translators, correspondents, collaborators, publishers including Patchen, production companies) are in regular upper and lower case letters.

Each section of the index is arranged in alphabetical order. The only exception is that where Patchen's name appears at the beginning of a title, the title is alphabetized under "P" even when his first name is the first word of the title.

INDEX
PART ONE

"The Known Soldier" A4a, A4b, A4c, A15, A34a, A34b
Knoxville News- Sentinel D58, D60

"The Lapper" A1a, A1b, A34a, A34b, D21
"The Lady-Faced Sows" A21a, A21b, A38a, A38b
"Lament and Lullaby" A20a, A20b, A20c, A27a, A27b
"Lament for the Makers of Songs" A18a, A18b, A19, A34a, A34b, D104
"A Lament for the Unlasting Joys" F5
"Land of the Never-Ending Heart" A13, A37
"Landscape of the Uneasy Soul" A8a, A8b
"The Landscapes of Paradise" D77
"Lao Tsze" A6a, A6b, A15, A34a, A34b
"La Porte de Salut est Large Sur le Village Qui Glisse a Travers le Soleil" D65
"La Renarde" D121
"The Last Full Measure of Devotion" A1a, A1b, A34a, A34b
"The Lasting Seasons" A4a, A4b, A4c, A15, A34a, A34b
"Last Years of the Poet Khiali" A6a, A6b, A15
"Late Summer Blues" A18a, A18b, A34a, A34b
La Voix de France D55
"Leaflet (One)" A1a, A1b, A34a, A34b, A37
"Leaflet (Two)" A1a, A1b, A34a, A34b, A37
"The Lean Ones of God are Clothed in Victories" D77
"Legend, For a Little Child" A5a, A5b, A34a, A34b
"Leighton Brewer, *Riders of the Sky*" D18
Le Journal des Poetes D121, D138
"Lenada" A4a, A4b, A4c, A9, A15, A34a, A34b
"Lenin" D9
Lesdain, Pierre D121
"Les Etoiles s'en Vont Dormir Si Paisiblement" D121
"Lessons for the Feast of Christmas" D202
"Let Me In" A27a, A27b, A34a, A34b
"Le Roi de Tenebres" D55
"A Letter on Liberty" A1a, A1b, A34a, A34b
"A Letter on Thanksgiving" A1a, A1b
"A Letter on the Use of Machine Guns at Weddings" A1a, A1b, A34a, A34b
"A Letter to a Distant Relative" A1a, A1b
"A Letter to Albion Moonlight" D51
"A Letter to a Policeman in Kansas City" A1a, A1b, A34a, A34b

"A Letter to God" A32a, A32b, A37, C3, D67
"A Letter to God: Star" D195
"A Letter to the Citizens of Tomorrow" A1a, A1b
"A Letter to the Inventors of a Tradition" A1a, A1b, A34a, A34b
"A Letter to the Liberals" A1a, A1b, A34a, A34b
"A Letter to the Young Men" A1a, A1b, A8a, A8b, A34a, A34b, D23
"Letter to the Young Men: II" D49
"A Letter to Those Who Are About to Die" A1a, A1b, A34a, A34b
"Let the World Be Any Man-Damned Way It Wants" D172
"Let Us Have Madness Openly" A1a, A1b, A8a, A8b, A10a, A10b, A10c, A19, A34a, A34b, D25
"Let Us Rejoice" A40a, A40b
"Letter to the Old Men" A1a, A1b, A34a, A34b, A37
Liberation D141, D143, D153, D154, D157, D158, D159, D161, D162, D164, D168, D169, D170, D174, D176, D179
"Lights are Going Out in the Castles" D35
"Like a Mourningless Child" A4a, A4b, A4c, A15, A34a, A34b
"Like I Told You" A26a, A26b
Limes Verlag A3g, A7f
"Limpidity of Silences" A10b, A10c, A20a, A20b, A20c, A27a, A27b, A34a, A34b
"The Lion Part" A33a, A33b, D161, D183
"The Lions of Fire Shall Have Their Hunting" A5a, A5b, A8a, A8b, A9, A10a, A10b, A10c, A34a, A34b, A37, D57, F3
"Lips Of The Angel" A6a, A6b, A15
""Listen" is a Purple Elephant" A25, A30
Literary Cavalcade D226
Literary Digest D25
"Little Bear" A4a, A4b, A4c, A15
"Little Birds Sit On Your Shoulders (For Miriam)" A27a, A27b, A31, A34a, A34b, F5
"The Little Black Train" A18a, A18b, A34a, A34b, D111, D118
"The Little Bug Angel" A25, A30
"Little Cannibal's Bedtimesong" A10b, A10c, A20a, A20b, A20c, A23, A27a, A27b, A34a, A34b
"Little Chief Son-Of-A-Gun-Don't-Give-A-Shoot" A33a, A33b, B14g, D213
"The Little Man Who Saw A Grass" A10b, A10c, A26a, A26b

INDEX
PART TWO

PS
3531   Morgan, Richard G.
A764   Kenneth Patchen

DATE			